TOMATOES

The American Horticultural Society
Illustrated Encyclopedia of Gardening

TOMATOES

The American Horticultural Society
Mount Vernon, Virginia

For The American Horticultural Society

President
Dr. Gilbert S. Daniels

Technical Advisory Committee
Everett Conklin
Mary Stuart Maury
Dr. John A. Wott

Tomatoes Staff for The Franklin Library/Ortho Books

Editorial Director
Min S. Yee

Supervisory Editor
Lewis P. Lewis

Editor
Ken Burke

Art Directors
John Williams
Barbara Ziller

Creative Director
Michael Mendelsohn

Assistant Creative Director
Clint Anglin

Written by
Walter L. Doty
A. Cort Sinnes

Contributing Writers
Annette C. Fabri
Susan M. Lammers

Illustrations by
Ron Hildebrand

Production Director
Robert Laffler

Production Manager
Renee Guilmette

Production Assistant
Paula Green

For Ortho Books

Publisher
Robert L. Iacopi

For The Franklin Library

Publisher
Joseph Sloves

The cover photograph shows two popular tomato varieties fresh from the garden. Top, 'Floramerica'; bottom, 'Tiny Tim'. Photograph © 1982 by Walter Chandoa.

Major Photography by
William Aplin
Clyde Childress
Michael Landis

Additional Photography by
Michael Lamotte
Fred Lyon
Tom Tracy

Acknowledgments

George Albers
Sangjo Han
John Mandry
Ted C. Torrey
W. Atlee Burpee Company

Wilbur C. Anderson
Robert A. Norton
Western Washington Research and Extension Unit

James R. Baggett
N. D. Mansour
Oregon State University

William M. Brooks
James D. Utzinger
Ohio State University

Samuel D. Cotner
Texas A&M University

John F. Gale
Stokes Seeds Inc.

Huts International
Phoenix, Arizona

Adel Kader
Charles Rick
Alan Stevens
University of California, Davis

John C. Kadon Associates
Scottsdale, Arizona

Victor Lambeth
University of Missouri

Raymond Lauber
Paul Thomas
James Waltrip
Colen Wyatt
Petoseed Company

Philip A. Minges
Cornell University—
State University of New York

Joseph Montelaro
Louisiana State University

Henri Perron
W. H. Perron & Co., Ltd.

Bernard J. Pollack
Rutgers—The State University of New Jersey

Gerald M. Sapers
U.S.D.A. Eastern Regional Research Center

Glenn Vincent
Park Seed Company

Allen Wilson
Goldsmith Seeds, Inc.

Charles B. Wilson
Harris Seed Company

Produced under the authorization of The American Horticultural Society by The Franklin Library and Ortho Books.

Library of Congress Catalog Card Number 82-71930

Printed in the United States of America

12 11 10 9 8 7 6 5 4 3 2 1

A Special Message from
The American Horticultural Society

The tantalizing, highly photogenic red of a vine-ripened tomato ready for harvest might be thought to imply the presence of a green thumb. We think that *Tomatoes* will lay to rest the green-thumb myth. The truth about that wizard with the miraculous hand is that the gardener simply observed, and put into practice, some basic and sensible truths about the plant and its growing habits. The fundamentals of this successful growing were based on the type of locale and its soils, the varieties best suited to that site, the climate, rainfall, and duration of the growing season, and the like. In its service as a guide to the grower, *Tomatoes* considers all of these ABCs.

The so-called "common" tomato is not all that common, despite its world-wide prestige as number one "vegetable" on the plates of peasants, poets, and kings. There's its "wild" side, the fruit's exotic beginnings in the tropics, its long intercontinental and transoceanic travel before attaining its present cultivated status. Such a trek denotes a certain sturdiness and survivability. We are not here concerned with some hothouse bloom, grown under glass and critical conditions, but a familiar fruit, or a variety thereof, best suited to your particular part of the planet.

No one interested in tomato growing need be deprived of its special enjoyment, whether you are an apartment dweller where space is at a premium but there are windowsills, or among the fortunate who have access to back lots and plots with acreage to spare. The key is the variety, and a large section in this book is devoted to a graphic presentation of more than a hundred tested and generally available regional specialities. There are few places in the continental United States where tomatoes will not flourish.

If the proof of it all is in the tasting, the harvest is just a beginning. We offer more than that wonderful, zesty mouthful of the seasoned raw slice. The tomato can make its presence known in many appetizing guises, and there's an abundance of recipes offered here to add to the adventure of good eating.

All in all, this excellent volume with clear text and profuse, appealing illustrations should be a welcome companion to all gardeners, neophyte and seasoned. It is written by experts; their experience can be part of yours.

Gilbert S. Daniels
President

CONTENTS

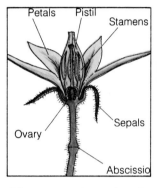

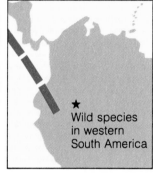

Here is an account of the "common" tomato with its rather exotic history of wandering and adapting before reaching today's status as a garden favorite. The anatomy of the tomato is dealt with in lucid and detailed illustrations. Frequently asked questions about troubles encountered in the growing of tomatoes are answered by experts.

Experts and beginners alike strive for the perfect tomato—in abundant harvest. By following the guidelines set down here, that target can be realized to a satisfying degree. This chapter covers the process from starting seeds and soil preparation to transplanting, feeding, and training. Home-greenhouse growers can utilize the commercial practices described.

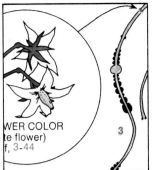 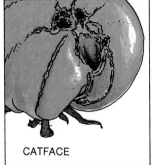 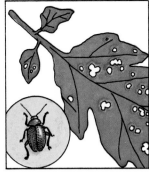

WER COLOR
e flower)
f, 3-44

3

CATFACE

Problems with Tomatoes 50

Totally carefree gardening is not yet within grasp, but trouble-shooting your tomato problems can be simplified with this illustrated discussion of tomato chromosomes, physiological disorders, pests, and diseases. A short but vital chapter dealing with the treatment and control of insects and diseases, from aphids to blossom-end rot to curly-top virus.

The Tomato's Relatives 58

It is an interesting surprise to learn that the tomato family includes a variety of plants: some common and popular vegetables, but some quite deadly. Specialized and expert advice is given as to proper care and growing procedures that can be useful to the gardener who finds room for Irish potatoes, eggplants, sweet and hot peppers, and more.

Cooking with Tomatoes 66

The fruits of a harvest can be a sublime adventure in taste, particularly when it's one of your own making. This specialized group of recipes glorifies the tomato: running the gamut from fish stews to spaghetti sauces, stuffed salads, antipasto, desserts, and side dishes. The logical and wonderful progression of vine to kitchen.

'Sweet-N-Early' (H Indeterminate Verticillium wilt Fusarium wilt	'Royal Chico'		58 days
'Starfire' (Standar Determinate			60 days

Tomato Varieties

If you're looking for that certain type of tomato, there's an excellent chance of finding it here. Over a hundred varieties of the tested and generally distributed tomatoes—profiles and portraits—are listed. The fourteen categories include early, mid-, and late season varieties as well as regional specialties. Availability as to seeds or small plants is noted.

TOMATOES

THE MOST POPULAR "VEGETABLE"

It has been a virtual odyssey for the tomato: from the New World to the Old and back to the New again, and from obscure origin to regal position on the international table.

A few things in the world still cannot be bought, and one of them is the incomparable taste of a truly fresh tomato. Its full flavor, fleshy texture, and juiciness set the vine-ripened tomato apart from its small, tough, translucent red counterpart found in the store.

Many people have made this taste discovery and have begun their own tomato gardens. Of 33 million gardening households in this country, 93 percent grow tomatoes. Without a doubt the tomato is the most popular "vegetable" grown today, although botanically it is really a fruit.

Everything tastes better when you raise it yourself. Growing your own allows you to enjoy the fruits of your labor at their peak. You can have the pleasure of walking out your back door to pick a tomato right from the vine. Rarely are your taste expectations so completely satisfied as when you bite into your first home-grown tomato of the season.

As the harvest season picks up, the kitchen becomes a most important extension of the garden. Suddenly menus begin to change, revolving around the juicy fresh tomatoes which abound in the garden. Salads become zestier and sauces richer; casseroles look and taste more delectable. Dinner during tomato season always includes a fresh vegetable. Finger foods can be picked right from the vine, and cooking becomes a challenge to your ingenuity. And you always have a welcome gift on hand for neighbors and friends who don't have gardens.

Tomatoes are a good source of vitamins and minerals, especially vitamins A and C. A 3½-ounce serving of raw tomato provides 1500 International Units of vitamin A (30% of the recommended daily allowance) and 25 milligrams of vitamin C (42% of the recommended daily allowance). Small amounts of other vitamins and minerals are present too. Unlike green vegetables, tomatoes lose very little of their nutrients in cooking.

Cooked tomatoes are used in omelets, stews, casseroles, meat sauces, salad dressings, and even breads. You can make your own tomato juice, create a secret spaghetti sauce, or make fresh cream of tomato soup.

Tomatoes are also excellent cooked as a single vegetable dish. Try them stewed, scalloped, stuffed and baked, or sliced and glazed in wine and brown sugar. For barbecues, skewer tomato slices and grill them quickly over the coals.

Because of the international background of the tomato in its journey of development, recipes that include the tomato are available from nearly every country of the world.

No matter where you live you can enjoy that special home-grown flavor. Tomatoes can be grown almost anyplace where the sun shines 6 to 7 hours a day—along sidewalks, beside walls, on rooftops, in barrels, and on your windowsill inside or outside. With just a few plants, a reasonable amount of time and energy, and the information in this book, you can produce an abundant harvest that will keep you supplied with tomatoes all season long.

Right: Fresh homemade tomato juice is both easy to make and delicious.

Bottom: Straight from the vine to the platter, tomatoes are a feast for both the palate and the eye.

But what makes the difference between the tomatoes sold in stores and the home-grown tomatoes your garden produces? The fact is: Good things happen to the flavor, color, juiciness, and texture of the tomato that is ripened on the vine. The same good things don't happen to the tomato that is ripened off the vine.

The number of days in the year that ripe fruit can be picked from vines in the garden is limited. The demand for tomatoes is year-round, however, and this demand is usually met. The problems of transportation, storage, and ripening have been reduced, but the fully ripe tomato still cannot be shipped. As stated in the United Fresh Fruit and Vegetable Association's bulletin on tomatoes: "The ideal tomato, from the consumer's viewpoint, is one that is full size, vine-ripened, unblemished, and characteristically at the red-ripe stage or anything near that stage. Such fruit is too tender even to stand commercial harvesting, let alone packing and shipping. (Note: So-called 'vine-ripe' tomatoes are not fully vine-ripe but are harvested at the turning or pink stage.) On the other hand, if a grower harvests tomatoes at the stage where they are most resistant to shipping injury, they lack juiciness and flavor."

A "mature-green" tomato has a glossy appearance, but no red color. The gel in the seed cavity is well formed, and the seeds slip off the edge of a sharp knife when the tomato is sliced.

Commercially grown tomatoes are considered vine-ripe when color begins to show at the blossom end. Whether mature-green or vine-ripe, tomatoes should be allowed to ripen fully for best flavor.

The best temperature range for ripening a tomato is 60° to 70°F. Flavor will be impaired when tomatoes are exposed to temperatures below 55°F. High temperatures (above 80°F.) also prevent good color and flavor, and increase the chance of decay.

Above, clockwise from top left: Tomatoes thriving in 6-inch pots hanging by a sunny window; checking for ripeness—the daily "treasure hunt"; these huge tomatoes are rough but full of flavor; beautifying this patio, tomatoes in containers make an unusual, welcome decoration; true to its name, this string of 'Sweet 100' will ripen to sweet perfection.

Left: Tomatoes ripen from the inside out.

Green tomatoes offer many culinary possibilities, not the least of which is green tomato pie.

Moderate light will speed ripening; too much sunlight prevents development of normal, even color.

Don't expect *immature* green tomatoes to ripen off the vine; they have a bitter taste and are likely to rot if kept for any length of time. When selecting green tomatoes for cooking, select those of mature size that would, under ordinary conditions, be about a week from turning red. (See description of mature-green tomatoes on the previous page.)

Unfortunately, taste is not the primary concern of commercial tomato breeders and growers. Instead, they must concentrate on developing those qualities that will sell tomatoes in the store. Tomatoes sold in the store are picked when they are green. Then they are cleaned, packed, and loaded onto trucks to make the trip to the store, sometimes across several states. California, for example, supplies the entire country with more than half the tomatoes sold each year.

As the tomatoes are transported, the ripening process begins. Of primary importance to the commercial grower is the tomato's ability to be shipped, its slow-ripening quality, and its esthetic appeal. Commercially grown tomatoes are tough-skinned and shapely so that they can weather the bruising trip to the market and still attract the shopper.

Only after the tomato is bought and in your kitchen does *taste* become a factor, and by that time the tomato is out of the hands of the seller and into yours.

Commercial growers and shippers do a good job, given their circumstances. They supply stores with fresh tomatoes every month of the year, and they grow enough tomatoes to be canned, frozen, and used in processed foods as well. However, the fact that they must produce on such a large scale and handle such massive quantities limits their ability to provide a product with the home-grown flavor of truly fresh tomatoes.

The only way to get that special flavor is to grow your own, but even that will not assure you of tomatoes superior to those in the store. The quality of your tomatoes will depend on how the many factors of growing come together.

Different standards apply to store-bought and home-grown tomatoes. To a home gardener, abnormal shapes, splits, holes, blemishes, and bruises are acceptable—but become a challenge. Taste and texture are the ultimate aims.

Plant Types

Tomato plants are either bushy or tall-growing (see illustrations on pages 15 and 16). The bushy or determinate plant is self-topping and grows to about 3 feet or less in height. The terminal buds set fruit, stopping the growth of the main stem. Since all the fruit form at about the same time, harvest is short (a week to 10 days). Determinate plants usually do not require staking or other support.

The tall-growing or indeterminate plant must be trained with stakes, a trellis, or a wire cage. Since terminal buds do not set fruit but result in the continued production of leaves and stems, the vine will grow indefinitely until killed by frost. The harvest period may last several months, with tomatoes at all stages of development on the vine at any one time.

Avoid trouble. Many areas are free from verticillium wilt, fusarium wilt, and nematodes, but, *if you have had trouble* growing tomatoes, plant the disease-resistant varieties.

End of the season. The end of the season is the time to take advantage of the pink, yellow, white, and green tomatoes that remain on the vine.

As one good gardener writes about his best method of storage at the end of the growing season: "We eat fresh tomatoes into December in spite of early October frosts. Just before the first frost, we tear the whole vine out of

Anatomy of the Tomato

Determinate Tomato

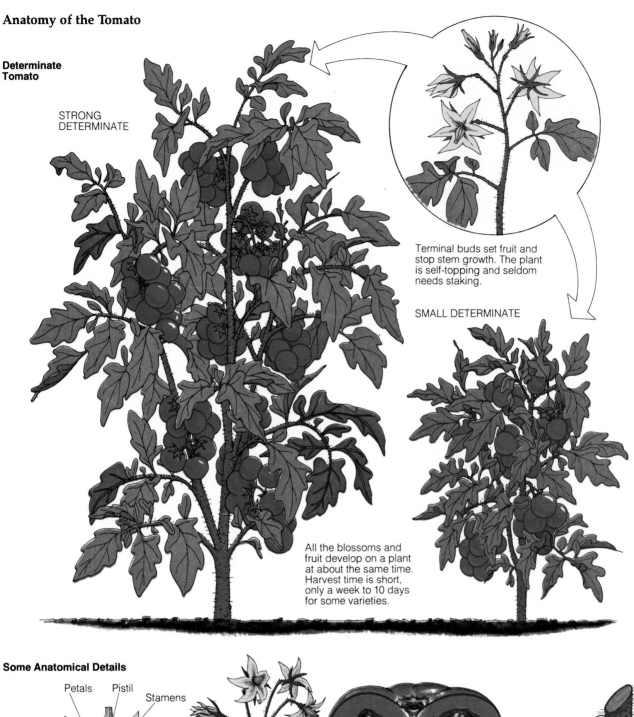

STRONG DETERMINATE

Terminal buds set fruit and stop stem growth. The plant is self-topping and seldom needs staking.

SMALL DETERMINATE

All the blossoms and fruit develop on a plant at about the same time. Harvest time is short, only a week to 10 days for some varieties.

Some Anatomical Details

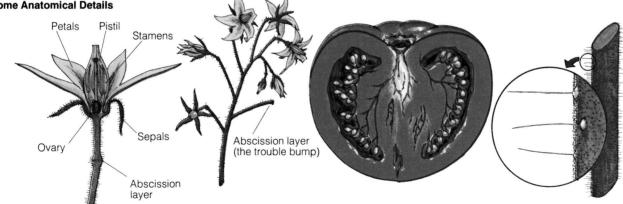

Petals Pistil Stamens

Ovary

Sepals

Abscission layer

Abscission layer (the trouble bump)

Tomato flowers are complete with both male and female organs and are mostly self-fertilizing. When fruit fails to set and blossoms drop, the abscission layer layer is where it separates (see page 20).

The fruit has two or more chambers called "locules." Large-fruited varieties have five to ten. A gelatin-like substance surrounds the seeds.

Glandular hairs are found on stems and leaves. When bent they give off the oil that gives tomatoes their characteristic odor.

Anatomy of the Tomato

Indeterminate Tomato

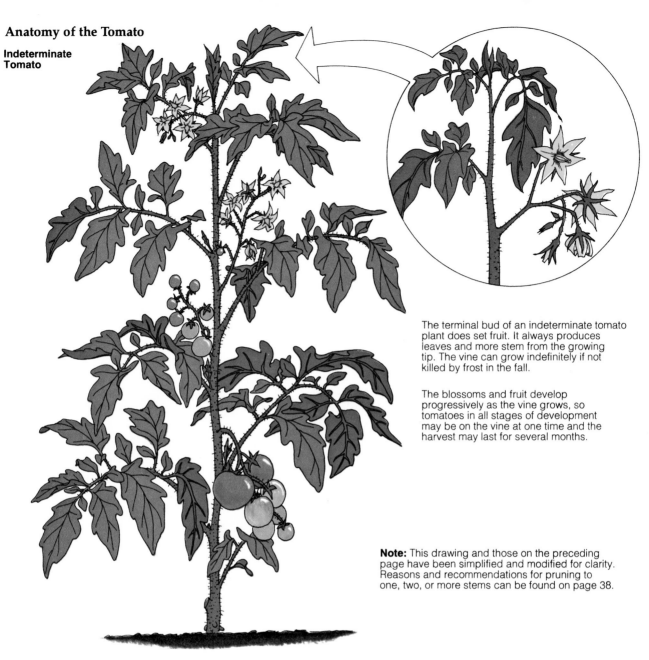

The terminal bud of an indeterminate tomato plant does set fruit. It always produces leaves and more stem from the growing tip. The vine can grow indefinitely if not killed by frost in the fall.

The blossoms and fruit develop progressively as the vine grows, so tomatoes in all stages of development may be on the vine at one time and the harvest may last for several months.

Note: This drawing and those on the preceding page have been simplified and modified for clarity. Reasons and recommendations for pruning to one, two, or more stems can be found on page 38.

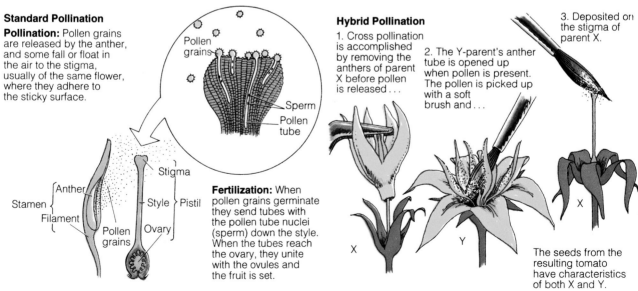

Standard Pollination

Pollination: Pollen grains are released by the anther, and some fall or float in the air to the stigma, usually of the same flower, where they adhere to the sticky surface.

Pollen grains

Sperm

Pollen tube

Stigma

Anther

Stamen

Filament

Style — Pistil

Pollen grains

Ovary

Fertilization: When pollen grains germinate they send tubes with the pollen tube nuclei (sperm) down the style. When the tubes reach the ovary, they unite with the ovules and the fruit is set.

Hybrid Pollination

1. Cross pollination is accomplished by removing the anthers of parent X before pollen is released . . .

2. The Y-parent's anther tube is opened up when pollen is present. The pollen is picked up with a soft brush and . . .

3. Deposited on the stigma of parent X.

X

Y

X

The seeds from the resulting tomato have characteristics of both X and Y.

the ground and hang it (actually eight to ten vines) upside down in the coldest part of our basement. This is the best method of post-frost storage I have run into. The fruits slowly ripen, and you pick them as they ripen."

Don't hang all the vines with green fruits upside down in the basement or garage to ripen or rot. Take some of the tomatoes directly into the kitchen. You will be rewarded with interesting new flavors and dishes.

Relishes and piccalillis can be made from them, and other tomato recipes will surprise you with their wholesome and distinctive flavors—pan-fried slices of green tomato, green tomato pie, and tomato-flavored breads will help you finish off the season in style.

The Tomato's Long Journey

The following brief, informal, up-to-date acccount of the origin of the cultivated tomato was prepared by Dr. Charles M. Rick. Dr. Rick, a professor in the Department of Vegetable Crops, University of California, Davis, works primarily on basic tomato genetics and is one of the leading authorities in this field.

Even when the season is over, tomatoes will continue to ripen on the vine when hung in a cool protected spot.

"The origin of the cultivated tomato is shrouded in mystery. Considering the perishability of all parts of the tomato plant, it isn't surprising that archaeology hasn't been much help in telling the story. However, we can piece together a story from what we know about the tomato historically— where it grew, who grew it, how it was used. And we also have helpful genetic evidence. The exact origin of the tomato may defy us, but we can work out a fairly reasonable conjecture.

"What, then, are the solid facts? First, the genus *Lycopersicon*—the botanical group to which the tomato belongs—is native to western South America, and only *Lycopersicon lycopersicum* var. *cerasiforme*, the wild cherry form of the cultivated species, has spread throughout Latin America and the New World Tropics. Second, the tomato was not known in Europe until *after* the discovery and conquest of America, descriptions and drawings first appearing in the European herbals of the middle and late 16th century. Third, these writings clearly reveal that man had been trying to improve the size of the tomato and the diversity of its shape and color. These improvements over the wild ancestors were almost certainly achieved by early man in America. Mexico appears to have been the site of domestication and the source of the earliest introductions, and the wild cherry tomato was probably the immediate ancestor.

"According to this hypothesis, wild, tiny, red-fruited tomatoes of Peruvian origin migrated northward through Ecuador, Colombia, Panama, and Central America to Mexico, where the migration seems to have stopped. We assume this because we have no evidence that North American Indians were acquainted with the tomato. In Mexico, man's continued selection for larger and more diverse fruits led to domestication. Recent research on hereditary characters of wild cherry tomatoes from this route reveals that some evolutionary changes occurred during the move north from Peru. We know this because genetic tests show that old European and many modern cultivars have the same genes as these migrant cherry types, but differ considerably from those of the wild and cultivated tomatoes from Peru and Ecuador.

"After the trip from Peru to Mexico, then where? [The map on the next page illustrates the wanderings of the tomato.] Introduction to Europe, possibly first in Spain, was followed by slow migration throughout the Mediterranean region, and later to northern Europe. The tomato was first grown as a curiosity, and for the ornamental value of its fruit. Its culinary use was delayed by fears of poisonous qualities. The tomato belongs to the nightshade family, which includes some plants of well-known toxicity. Because of its association with them, people were afraid to eat tomatoes, a

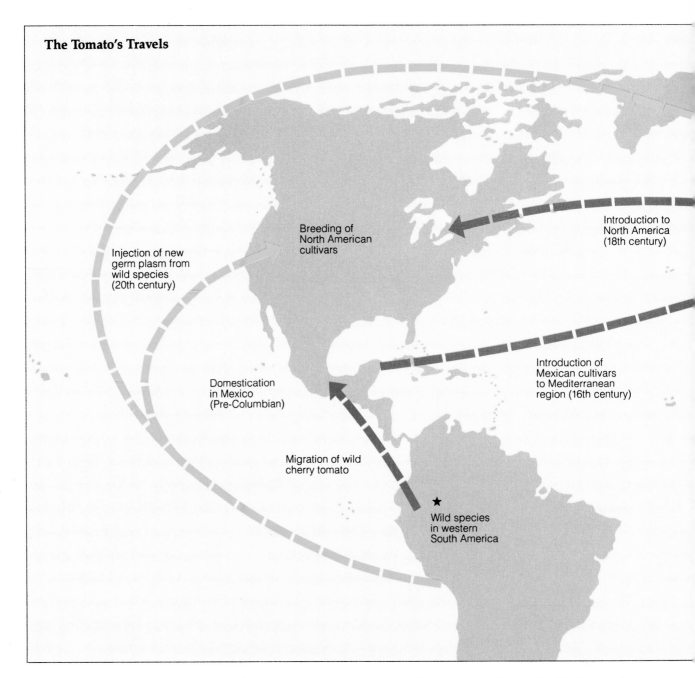

Injection of new
germ plasm from
wild species
(20th century)

Breeding of
North American
cultivars

Introduction to
North America
(18th century)

Introduction of
Mexican cultivars
to Mediterranean
region (16th century)

Domestication
in Mexico
(Pre-Columbian)

Migration of wild
cherry tomato

★
Wild species
in western
South America

fear that persisted even into this century—long after its food value was
discovered by the Italians and other Europeans.

"As was the potato (also of American origin), the tomato was reintro-
duced to the New World from Europe. In the United States the tomato was
of minor importance until the middle 1800s, although Thomas Jefferson was
growing it in the late 18th century. The first known attempts to breed
improved types date from 1860. Until the turn of the century, most of the
improvement resulted from selection within existing stocks, mainly of
French origin. As the tomato gained importance as a food plant, breeding
efforts accelerated, with extensive hybridization and selection. Until quite
recently, breeders limited their efforts to working with European stocks as
parent plants. These proved to be restricted sources when the need arose for
disease and pest resistance and for other characteristics not present in European stocks. Breeders then exploited genes in primitive cultivars and wild
species from the native region. The resistance to fusarium and verticillium
wilt and to nematodes, now incorporated in many cultivars, is the product
of such efforts."

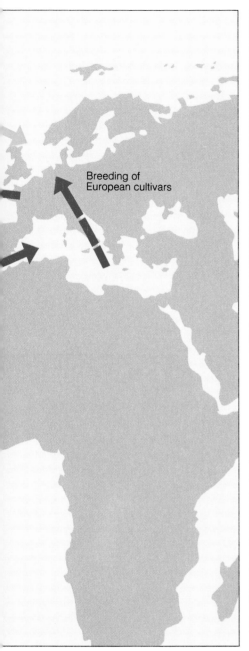

Breeding of
European cultivars

The supposed ancestor of all modern tomato varieties is *Lycopersicon lycopersicum* var. *cerasiforme*. Top left: The plant. Top right: The flowers. Above: The fruit.

Questions About Growth Habits

Even the gardener who grows prize-winning carrots, beets, chard, beans, and even cauliflower may sometimes have trouble growing tomatoes. The tomato is not always a solid citizen of the garden. When all growth factors are right, it produces magnificently. At other times it fails miserably. The sensitive behavior of the tomato plant has led to speculation about every stage in its development.

The late Dr. Philip Minges, who taught at Cornell University, gave the following answers to the questions most frequently asked about tomatoes. His answers are in quotes. Answers without quotes are based on the research and experience of others.

Why do blossoms drop? Many of the main-season tomato varieties will set fruit only within a rather narrow range of night temperatures.

Temperatures above 55°F. for at least part of the night are required for the first fruit set. Night temperatures above 75°F. in the summer months inhibit fruit set; that is, they cause the blossoms to drop. Most of the early-

If tomato flowers are not fertilized with their own pollen in the critical 50 hours after blooming, they will not fruit. Instead, the flowers drop, which is usually a result of too high or too low night temperatures.

season varieties will set fruit at lower temperatures, and plant breeders have developed varieties that will continue to set fruit at night temperatures above 75°F.

Every section of the country has good and bad years for growing tomatoes. Spring weather may be erratic, abnormally cold, and wet. A heat wave may come along in July to knock the blossoms off.

To many a gardener the most critical hours in the life of a tomato plant is the time when it is setting fruit. The blossoms are out. Will they drop off or set fruit? The gardener must wait about 50 hours from the time a blossom appears to find out. It takes that long or longer for the pollen to germinate and the pollen tube to grow down the pistil to the ovary. At night temperatures below 55°F., pollen germination and tube growth are so slow the blossoms drop off before they are fertilized.

Why is a plant all vine and no fruit? It is often said that, given too much nitrogen and water in the early stages, a tomato plant will produce foliage at the expense of fruit.

That statement is incorrect.

No one can question the fact that a heavy application of nitrogen and water *will* produce vigorous vine growth—but it isn't the whole story, as scientists have pointed out.

Actually, here's what happens. Once the flowers set, the plant takes care of itself. If you feed it lots of nitrogen and flowers don't set, then you get a lot of vine growth. But nitrogen is not responsible for a tomato plant's failing to change gears from the vegetative to the fruiting state.

Here's an example of "all vine and no fruit" in one garden, which had two plants of 'Fantastic', two of 'Delicious', and two of 'Yellow Plum'. The gardener was picking ripe fruit from the first blossom cluster of 'Fantastic'. All the early blossoms of 'Delicious' had dropped, and fruit was setting on flowers—at five feet above the ground. The 'Yellow Plum' was at seven feet and producing from the *ground up*.

What's the explanation? Night temperature—not too much nitrogen. Fertilizer treatments were the same on all three varieties. Evidently, the 'Delicious' needs a higher night temperature than the 'Fantastic' for first blossom set. In this garden, 'Delicious' was a beautiful vine with two green fruits, and maybe more to come.

Can fruit set be improved? Pollen is shed most abundantly on bright sunny days between 10 A.M. and 4 P.M. Shedding occurs within individual flowers. Tapping or jarring the entire plant is effective only when the flower clusters

Left: Flowers that have been pollinated, as well as the fruits that will follow, are firmly attached to the plant.

Right: Ripe tomatoes are easily removed by giving them a slight twist which causes a break at the node.

are near the top of the plant. To increase pollination over the whole plant, give individual attention to all flower clusters with daily vibration, using an electric vibrator or battery-operated toothbrush. The best time to shake and vibrate plants is at midday when the air is warm and the humidity is low.

Does sprinkling knock flowers off tomatoes and other vegetables? "No, not unless the flowers were about to fall off anyway. When flowers fail to set, in a few days an abcission layer forms at a node, as with leaves in autumn, and in a week or so they will drop off. Fertilized flowers and fruits remain well secured to the plants so that it is almost impossible to pull or knock them off (though there is an occasional exception)."

Will sprinkling in hot weather cause leaf burn? "No. If anything, the plants will be cooled and the transpiration rate will drop."

Will crowding tomato plants reduce fruit size? "Usually not enough to be perceptible. Crowding of this group of vegetables usually reduces the yield per plant rather than the size of the fruit. Adequate soil moisture during the fruit-growing period is the major factor for obtaining normal size of fruit."

Will pruning tomatoes help or hinder good yield? "Tomato yields per plant may be lowered by pruning. Removing the leaves or shoots does not conserve 'food' for the crop; it tends to reduce the total food supply. With certain methods of staking, some pruning is necessary, but when it is possible, use training methods that require little pruning."

Is direct sunlight necessary for ripening tomatoes? "No. Tomatoes will turn color and ripen in shade or in the dark at proper temperatures. In fact, red or pink tomatoes will turn yellow on the exposed side if they receive too much sun, so some foliage cover is beneficial. Dense foliage late in the summer or early fall may retard ripening because of lowering the fruit temperature."

What causes holes, streaks, and deformities in tomato fruit? "This disorder might be called 'blossom-tear.' It is a growth defect that begins shortly after the setting of a fruit. Blossom-tear seems to occur most frequently when wet, cool weather prevails during the flowering period, causing the corolla (yellow part of the flower) to stick to the small ovary. As the ovary expands, the corolla eventually breaks loose, tearing away a small amount of wall tissue. The hole enlarges as the fruit grows. Blossom-tear basically harms only the appearance of the tomato. No control has been discovered."

What causes blotchiness in tomatoes, and how can it be controlled? "The cause is not clearly understood, and there is no consistently satisfactory

A "zipper" streak on a beefsteak-type tomato is no cause for alarm—it affects only the appearance, not taste.

control. Blotchiness is a physiological disorder characterized by lack of red pigment and hard tissue. (Sometimes dark or black strands appear in the white, or greenish, abnormal tissue.) It may be visible externally or apparent only after cutting the fruit. You can use fruits with a small or moderate amount of blotchy tissue, but badly affected fruits are culls. Though no varieties are immune, some tend to be less affected than others. For example, 'Heinz 1350' is a less susceptible variety."

What defines a tomato's quality? The quality of a tomato of any variety is not an inherent characteristic. Quality of the individual fruits depends on a total of all the factors that contribute to the plant's growth: sunlight, soil, moisture supply, nutrient supply, methods of cultivation, and exposure—all play a part in determining the ultimate quality of the fruit. Tests made by Cornell University on the variety 'New Yorker' show that, within a mile or two, its quality will vary slightly from garden to garden.

Should a gardener worry about leaf rolling on tomatoes? "In most cases there are no diseases or other disorders involved, and yields are not affected. On many varieties, after a good load of fruit has set, the lower leaves begin to roll up, or cup. We've found that the greater the ratio of fruit to leaf area, the more the leaves will roll. Varieties with a lower ratio of fruit to leaf area have less leaf roll. Poor-yielding varieties have less roll. Pruning off leaves and shoots will intensify rolling—as will a moisture shortage. A few varieties have a genetic tendency for 'rolling characteristic.' These will often exhibit leaf rolling even before any fruit sets."

Why do potatoes sometimes produce tomatoes? "They don't. Some years, potato flowers set to produce potato seed balls, which resemble tomatoes."

Intergeneric grafting is possible within the nightshade family. On one very strange-looking plant, eggplant, pepper, tomato, and petunia have been grafted.

Should tomato seed be saved? If you want to perpetuate a *standard* variety of tomatoes that has performed well in your garden, save seed from some of its fruits. However, if you're planning on saving seed of any of the *hybrids*, you should know this: The first season you plant the seed of 'Better Boy', or any other hybrid, you will get a duplication of 'Better Boy', or whatever hybrid you planted. But hybrid seed is genetically stable for only one season. After that, you may get six different varieties from six seeds.

In the list of varieties beginning on page 114 we note whether the variety is a hybrid (H) variety, which will not breed true from seed.

These lush strings of 'Sweet 100' don't ripen all at once. They supply the gardener with a continuous crop of sweet cherry-type tomatoes.

GROWING TOMATOES

A green thumb at the start is not a requirement for a final harvested beauty. But careful observance of tomato-growing fundamentals can ensure a successful crop.

Everyone wants perfect tomatoes. The tomato plant will deliver them if it gets what it needs. It needs what every plant needs—and more. The six fundamental requirements of the tomato are:

1. *A continuous and uniform supply of water.* Water neither too much nor too little. Too much water can drown a plant, especially if the roots are in a heavy soil. Too little water can stop tomato production.
2. *A continuous supply of nutrients.* The plant's daily nutrient requirement is small, but that amount should be available when the plant needs it. Always follow package or bottle directions for best results.
3. *Air in the soil after drainage.* This factor is the most important one in the growth of plants. Roots breathe. Deprived of air, roots, or portions of roots, die of suffocation. Make sure soil is loose and friable, permitting good drainage.
4. *Sunlight.* To a plant, light is life. Sunlight is used by the leaves to convert raw materials into usable plant food and to provide the energy required for photosynthesis. The tomato should have 8 hours of continuous sunlight but can get along with less. See page 49.
5. *Temperature.* Most tomatoes need night temperatures between 55° and 75°F. to set fruit. Some varieties will set fruit at lower or higher temperatures. See pages 114 to 138.
6. *Protection of leaves and roots.* Leaves and roots need protection from temperature extremes, strong winds, birds and other animals, weed competition, and pests and diseases. But if the first five requirements have been satisfied, the plant should be strong enough to withstand any damage and will require much less protection from the gardener.

One need not be a horticulturist to grow tomatoes or to follow rules for good plant growth. Insufficient concern for one or more of the needs of the plant is what trips up many gardeners. Actually, these six fundamentals are one fundamental; *all* must be observed.

You can go into the garden, look at a tomato plant, and decide that it needs more fertilizer. Fine. But also bear in mind that fertilizing, the nature of the soil in which the tomato vine is planted, and your watering habits are all interdependent.

If a six-pack of the tomato variety recommended by your garden store is planted, and all grow and produce well, this is fortunate—perhaps lucky. But if the experience hasn't been highly successful, the following pages of advice may be helpful.

Starting from Scratch

The trick in sowing seeds indoors is timing, with the goal of setting out an ideal-size transplant when the weather is just right. Seed germination should take 5 to 7 days; and from 5 to 6 weeks to grow to transplant size. That

The One-Step Method

Choose containers, any of those illustrated on page 29, except flats. We've found peat cubes or Jiffy-7s are the easiest to work with.

Sow seed by putting two in each dampened container.

Wire wickets

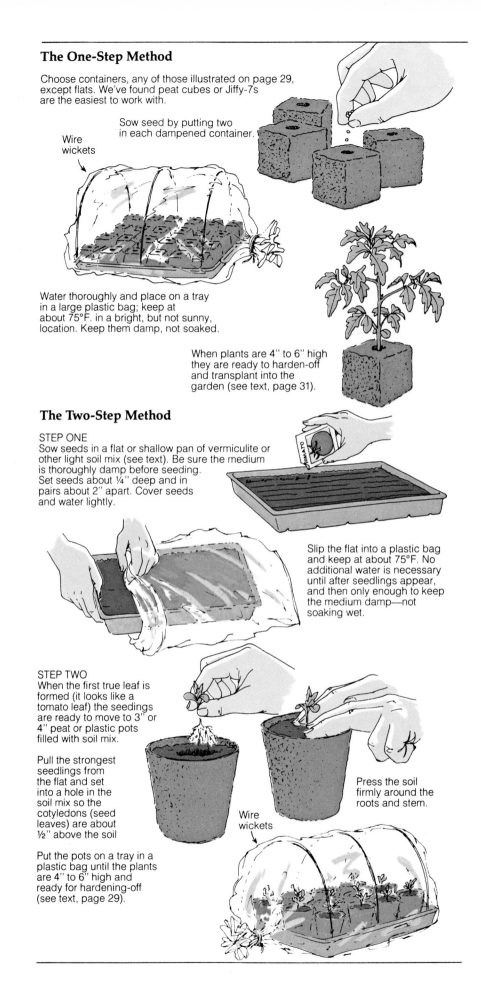

Water thoroughly and place on a tray in a large plastic bag; keep at about 75°F. in a bright, but not sunny, location. Keep them damp, not soaked.

When plants are 4" to 6" high they are ready to harden-off and transplant into the garden (see text, page 31).

The Two-Step Method

STEP ONE
Sow seeds in a flat or shallow pan of vermiculite or other light soil mix (see text). Be sure the medium is thoroughly damp before seeding. Set seeds about ¼" deep and in pairs about 2" apart. Cover seeds and water lightly.

Slip the flat into a plastic bag and keep at about 75°F. No additional water is necessary until after seedlings appear, and then only enough to keep the medium damp—not soaking wet.

STEP TWO
When the first true leaf is formed (it looks like a tomato leaf) the seedings are ready to move to 3" or 4" peat or plastic pots filled with soil mix.

Pull the strongest seedlings from the flat and set into a hole in the soil mix so the cotyledons (seed leaves) are about ½" above the soil

Press the soil firmly around the roots and stem.

Wire wickets

Put the pots on a tray in a plastic bag until the plants are 4" to 6" high and ready for hardening-off (see text, page 29).

means sowing the seed 6 to 8 weeks prior to the optimum planting time in your area. Eight to twelve plants should be enough to provide the average household with both fresh tomatoes and tomatoes for canning. Since seed and planting materials are relatively inexpensive, start with more peat pots than are absolutely needed. The increase in cost is minute, but the practice may make the difference between failure and success. There might not be 100% germination—and some seedlings might not make the grade to transplant size.

Direct seeding. Direct seeding may be into 3- or 4-inch clay or peat pots or some of the newer plant-growing containers. Fill the pots to about ½ inch from the top with a sterilized potting medium. Plant one to three seeds ⅓- to ½-inch deep in the center of each pot. Plant at a uniform depth so seeds will germinate evenly and result in uniform plants for transplanting into the beds. After germination, thin seedlings to one per pot. Cut off the tops of the seedlings you don't need. Don't pull them; that will disturb the one you're saving.

Whether in trays, cubes, or some other container, the material should be thoroughly moist before seeds are sown. Give them the warmest spot available. For fast germination, tomato seeds need a soil temperature of 75° to 85°F.

Cover blocks or peat pots or trays with paper or slip them into a plastic bag to prevent drying out. Further watering is not needed until the seeds have sprouted.

Once the seedlings emerge, they should be kept in full sunlight—for 12 hours a day if possible. The temperatures for seedling growth should be between 70° and 75°F. during the day and between 60° and 65°F. during the night.

Easily constructed small greenhouses.

Vigorous seedlings can be started indoors using artificial light.

Three fully ripe tomatoes cluster temptingly on the vine.

To Keep Seedlings Warm and Moist

Warming cable. When spread beneath the soil in a flat, it provides gentle, uniform heat for quick seed germination and optimum plant growth.

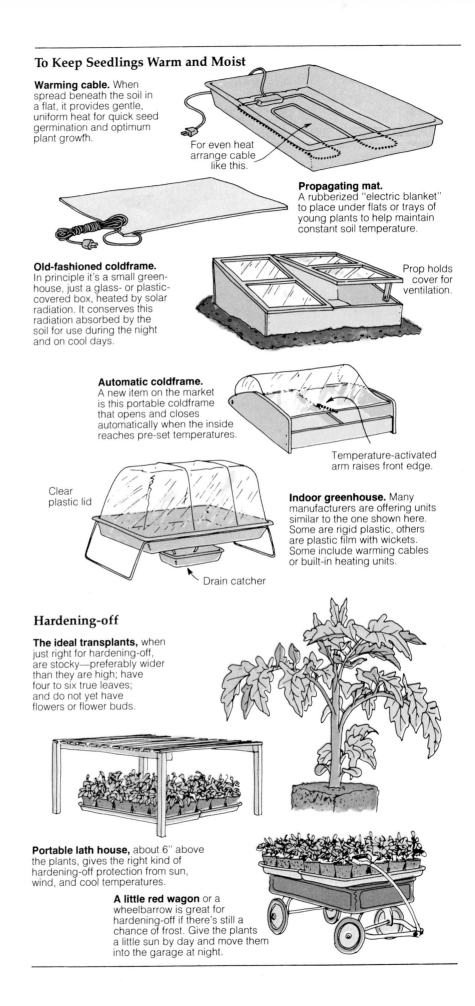

For even heat arrange cable like this.

Propagating mat. A rubberized "electric blanket" to place under flats or trays of young plants to help maintain constant soil temperature.

Old-fashioned coldframe. In principle it's a small greenhouse, just a glass- or plastic-covered box, heated by solar radiation. It conserves this radiation absorbed by the soil for use during the night and on cool days.

Prop holds cover for ventilation.

Automatic coldframe. A new item on the market is this portable coldframe that opens and closes automatically when the inside reaches pre-set temperatures.

Temperature-activated arm raises front edge.

Clear plastic lid

Indoor greenhouse. Many manufacturers are offering units similar to the one shown here. Some are rigid plastic, others are plastic film with wickets. Some include warming cables or built-in heating units.

Drain catcher

Hardening-off

The ideal transplants, when just right for hardening-off, are stocky—preferably wider than they are high; have four to six true leaves; and do not yet have flowers or flower buds.

Portable lath house, about 6" above the plants, gives the right kind of hardening-off protection from sun, wind, and cool temperatures.

A little red wagon or a wheelbarrow is great for hardening-off if there's still a chance of frost. Give the plants a little sun by day and move them into the garage at night.

The many ways to start from seed. The containers used for the seed can be anything that will hold soil. To get the best results, however, follow these simple guidelines:

☐ For fast germination, grow the seed in temperatures of 70° to 80°F.
☐ Use a sterilized planter mix.
☐ Sow seed 6 to 8 weeks before time to set out plants—after the weather has stabilized.
☐ For best results, plant in biodegradable containers that can go directly in the ground, container and all. Use, for example, peat pots, Jiffy-7s, Kys Kubes, or other compressed peat containers.
☐ Move seedlings from flats to pots when first true leaves form.

Transplanting

While the accepted advice on handling transplants is excellent in theory, it is difficult to follow in the ordinary tomato-growing practices.

For example, the ideal transplant is described as a plant with four to six true leaves, wider than it is tall, stocky, young, and succulent. This plant should not be fresh from the greenhouse but should be slightly "hardened" by subjecting it to outdoor conditions. Such exposure will firm up the plant tissues, allowing the plant to withstand unfavorable environmental conditions. Buying that ideal or producing it at just the right time for outdoor planting is not always possible.

The bedding-plant grower has a series of target dates. The grower tries to deliver the ideal transplant for the early-planting customers and all those who follow throughout the transplant season. If the target date turns out too cold and rainy for any kind of gardening, either the bedding-plant grower or the retailer will have plants on hand that may be a week or two older before they are sold.

Containers for Seed Starting

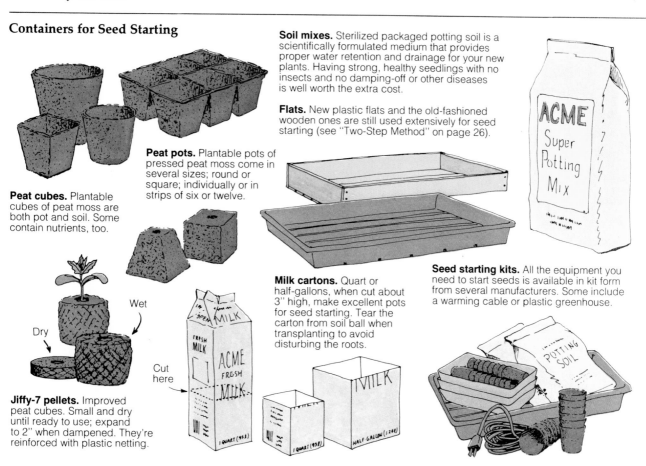

Soil mixes. Sterilized packaged potting soil is a scientifically formulated medium that provides proper water retention and drainage for your new plants. Having strong, healthy seedlings with no insects and no damping-off or other diseases is well worth the extra cost.

Flats. New plastic flats and the old-fashioned wooden ones are still used extensively for seed starting (see "Two-Step Method" on page 26).

Peat pots. Plantable pots of pressed peat moss come in several sizes; round or square; individually or in strips of six or twelve.

Peat cubes. Plantable cubes of peat moss are both pot and soil. Some contain nutrients, too.

Jiffy-7 pellets. Improved peat cubes. Small and dry until ready to use; expand to 2" when dampened. They're reinforced with plastic netting.

Wet

Dry

Cut here

Milk cartons. Quart or half-gallons, when cut about 3" high, make excellent pots for seed starting. Tear the carton from soil ball when transplanting to avoid disturbing the roots.

Seed starting kits. All the equipment you need to start seeds is available in kit form from several manufacturers. Some include a warming cable or plastic greenhouse.

If the plants are in six-packs, the stems of the plants are only about 1½ inches apart. The chances of plants being wider than they are tall are remote. If sales are delayed at the retail outlet, the plant will be tall and spindly. Gardeners who insist on transplants at the earliest hint of summer weather are asking for trouble. The bedding-plant grower and the informed nursery owner know that planting before the weather has settled is risky.

Assume that indoors, or in your greenhouse, the young plant has grown past the ideal size for transplant and has moved into the flowering and fruit stage before the weather is right for planting in the garden. Won't there be earlier fruit production from that plant than from a fresh young transplant?

The answers are "yes" and "no." The "yes" answers come from growers who feed the transplant liberally throughout its stay in the greenhouse and give it the root space of a 6-inch pot. The "no" answers come from those who have tested the effect of age of transplants without qualifications.

Tests showed that growing plants 3 to 4 weeks longer in the greenhouse seldom shortens the time to the mature-ripe fruiting stage by more than a few days.

The reason for getting the transplant into its permanent location in its youthful stage is this: If you allow the transplant to flower and set fruit and then plant it in the garden, it will not have enough roots, at the time, to support the fruit. Even in a greenhouse operation, you're better off to move the ideal-size transplant into a 5-gallon container, if you want a good yield of fruit.

An experienced tomato grower had a different answer: "Yes, you can move out an overgrown transplant if you take these precautions." He gave the transplant the root space of a 6-inch pot and enough bench space for the leaves to spread. During its stay in the greenhouse the transplant was fed regularly. When the overgrown transplant went into the garden, it was fed again. Growth continued with little interruption.

A "no" rating came from another experiment—a test report on transplanting tomatoes when the fruits were the size of marbles.

Transplants held in the greenhouse until fruits of marble size had developed were planted in the garden in this fashion: Half of the plants were set out with the fruits on the vine; all of the fruits were removed from the other half.

The plants with fruit left on the vine ripened the already existing fruits—and then quit. The vines with the fruits removed continued to develop and produce a succession of crops.

The answer to the question, "Can you substitute time in the greenhouse for time outdoors in the garden?" is this: Yes, if you transplant the seedling to a large container (5-gallon size or larger) and transfer the container plant outdoors when the weather is right. Gardeners in areas where the season is too short or too cool for the late-season varieties manage to grow the late 'Beefsteak' variety in this fashion.

So the best answer still remains "yes" and "no."

Soil

For gardeners blessed with a soil that is deep and fertile, easy to work, and easy to manage, any remarks in this section about soil are not pertinent. But most tomato growers find themselves contending with problem soils ranging from too sandy to heavy clay. True, the tomato plant will thrive in heavy clay soil if you water *infrequently* but *deeply*. Making heavy soils more friable by adding organic matter may not make a big difference in the life of the tomato but it does make a difference in the life of the gardener.

The addition of organic matter—compost, peat moss, manure, sawdust, ground bark—makes clay soils more mellow and easier to work. Organic matter opens up tight clay soils, improves drainage, and allows air to move more readily through the soil, warming it up earlier in the spring. In light,

How to Transplant

Preparing the soil. Level and smooth your tomato patch. Spread organic matter and a good pelleted tomato food over the planting area. (Be sure to follow the directions on the label. They will tell you how many pounds for each 100 square feet.) Dig them in to a depth of 8 to 10 inches.

Digging holes. Mark where you want each plant and dig the hole deep enough to bury the tomato stem as far as the first leaf.

Starter solution. Soak each hole with a cup or so of high-phosphorus starter solution about ½-hour before planting. No additional fertilizer will be needed until after the fruit sets.

Ready the plant. If the plant is in a peat pot, tear the top edge off so it can't act as a wick and dry out the rootball.

If the plant is in a plastic, fiber, or clay pot, tip it out—don't pull it by the stem.

If the plant is in a peat cube it's ready to be put into the ground—cube and all.

Plant it deep. Put a good stocky plant in so the first leaf is just above the soil.

Leggy plants should be buried very deep. Pull off a few leaves and, to make planting easier, bend the stem and lay it in sideways.

Roots will develop all along the buried stem.

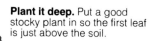

Firm the soil. Press the soil firmly around the rootball. Then water lightly to settle the soil and remove any air pockets that may be left around the rootball.

sandy soils, organic matter holds moisture and nutrients in the root zone. The more organic matter added to a sandy soil, the more its moisture-holding capacity is increased.

The quantity of organic matter must be large enough to change the structure of the soil physically. "Enough" means that at least one-third of the final mix is organic matter. To add this amount, spread over the soil a layer of organic matter at least 2 inches thick and work it in to a depth of 6 inches. Soil structure cannot be changed beneficially with a little dab of anything. (A word of caution: If peat moss is added to condition the garden soil, moisten the peat moss *before* mixing it into the soil. Wetting peat moss is not easy. One method is by putting the required amount in a plastic bag, adding warm water, and then squeezing and mixing the bag by hand.)

The total area of soil for eight to twelve vines—early and midseason varieties—will probably be relatively small.

Planting methods. One of two planting methods is suggested:

1. If the plants are to be trained on a trellis, condition the soil in a trench about 3 feet wide and 14 feet long. This trench will serve seven plants. Spread one 4-cubic-foot bag of peat moss and 4 cubic feet of vermiculite or perlite over the 3 × 14-foot area. After roughly mixing peat moss and vermiculite or perlite, 2 pounds of 5–10–10 dry fertilizer are sprinkled evenly over the area.

   All are then mixed into the soil. Use a tiller that mixes to a depth of 6 to 8 inches.
2. If the tomatoes are to be planted in cages, condition the soil only in the circle in which the tomatoes will grow.

   Although a tomato plant will grow in a soil that is slow to drain, too frequent watering clogs such soil and causes trouble. Gardeners with poor watering habits should grow tomatoes in a soil that cannot be waterlogged.

Soil tests. Acid soils that are ideal for rhododendrons and azaleas are not the best soils for tomatoes.

For gardeners wishing to grow the perfect tomato, the information provided by a soil test is essential.

The pH level and the lime requirement are by far the most important items in a soil test. The tomato plant requires a pH level of 6.0 to 7.0 for best growth.

Gardeners living in areas where the liming of lawns is a yearly affair can be sure that their natural soil is low in calcium—an element needed by the tomato to combat blossom-end rot.

Those who have had this problem should add 5 pounds of pulverized limestone to 100 square feet of soil before planting. Mix thoroughly throughout the top 8 to 12 inches of soil. Limestone adds calcium to the soil.

Many states offer free or low-cost soil tests. See your County Extension Agent for details. And see the section on "Containers and Hanging Baskets," page 44, for use of synthetic soil mixes in container gardening.

Plant Protection

The protection of young tomato plants from the vagaries of springtime weather is carried out in many ways—from the time-honored Hotkap to a parade of home-garden devices using sheets of clear plastic, recycled plastic jugs, coffee cans, and other items.

All devices are based on the principle of trapping the heat from the sun during the day and slowing the reradiation of that heat at night.

Heat build-up is a danger when using any protection device made of paper or clear plastic. Whatever device you use, be sure you provide for air circulation. A sudden change in the weather from gray clouds to bright

It's easy to transform an ordinary plastic bucket into a mini-greenhouse. Just poke a few holes to provide good air circulation.

sunlight has cooked many plants by building up temperatures inside an unventilated covering.

The tomato responds to night temperature in terms of the number of hours of darkness when temperatures are from 45° to 55°F. or above. If a cold night is predicted, gardeners can take advantage of the *higher* temperatures of the *first* hours of darkness by slowing the reradiation of heat from the soil.

This control can be accomplished by covering a raised bed of tomatoes with a sheet of fiberglass (see illustration), and comparing hourly temperatures beneath the panel with the outdoor temperatures until midnight. Temperatures beneath the panel are usually from 4° to 10°F. higher than those outdoors. The spread in temperatures is due to variations in wind velocity. Tomatoes grown under the fiberglass panel are larger, better-looking plants than any grown in the open. To the painstaking gardener, with only a dozen plants to care for, no step in plant protection is "too much trouble."

If strong winds are common, wind protection will increase the growth and the yield of the tomato plant. When the plant is under stress from wind, its growth processes are slowed down, with a resultant reduction in setting and bearing of fruit.

In areas where the first frost of fall is followed by a stretch of warm weather, plastic tents are used to extend the harvest by another 2 or 3 weeks.

Where rainfall is excessive for the best growth of tomatoes and other vegetables, the roof of fiberglass panels solves the rainy season problems for the plants. Constantly moist soil prevents the tomato plant from setting its first fruit. Therefore, letting the ground dry thoroughly between waterings is important in all cases.

A plastic bucket used to protect young tomato plants growing in plastic mulch.

Frost Protection for Transplants

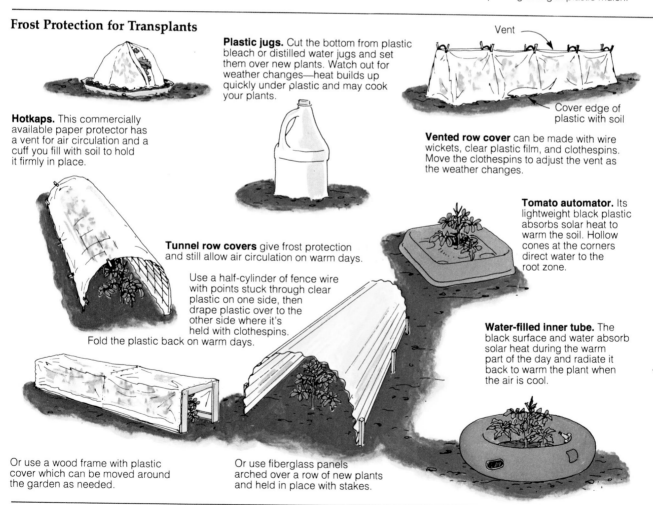

Hotkaps. This commercially available paper protector has a vent for air circulation and a cuff you fill with soil to hold it firmly in place.

Plastic jugs. Cut the bottom from plastic bleach or distilled water jugs and set them over new plants. Watch out for weather changes—heat builds up quickly under plastic and may cook your plants.

Vent

Cover edge of plastic with soil

Vented row cover can be made with wire wickets, clear plastic film, and clothespins. Move the clothespins to adjust the vent as the weather changes.

Tunnel row covers give frost protection and still allow air circulation on warm days.

Use a half-cylinder of fence wire with points stuck through clear plastic on one side, then drape plastic over to the other side where it's held with clothespins. Fold the plastic back on warm days.

Tomato automator. Its lightweight black plastic absorbs solar heat to warm the soil. Hollow cones at the corners direct water to the root zone.

Water-filled inner tube. The black surface and water absorb solar heat during the warm part of the day and radiate it back to warm the plant when the air is cool.

Or use a wood frame with plastic cover which can be moved around the garden as needed.

Or use fiberglass panels arched over a row of new plants and held in place with stakes.

Feeding

Home gardeners take care of the nutrient needs of the tomato in many ways. Every type of product is used—fish fertilizer, blood meal, hoof and horn meal, manure, and commercial liquid and dry fertilizers.

Before using any fertilizer, it is important to understand the labels on the bags and packages, whether they are labeled tomato food or given another name.

All commercial fertilizers are labeled by the percentages of nitrogen (N), phosphorus (P), and potassium (K) they contain. Many formulas will work.

N–P–K	N–P–K
4–12–2	5–10–10
6–20–10	6–18–6
18–24–6	18–18–21
10–10–10	and so on

The listings are always in the same order, with nitrogen first, phosphorus second, potassium third. The percentage of nitrogen in the formula dictates the amount of fertilizer to be applied. If the fertilizer being used has a higher percentage of nitrogen, less fertilizer is required. For example, if a 5–10–10 fertilizer is being used and there is a switch to one with a 10–10–10 formula, only half as much is needed. Gardeners who do not read directions and note the percentages on the package may inadvertently double or triple the amount of nitrogen that should be applied.

Remember, whenever using fertilizer, don't try to out-guess the manufacturer. Read the label, and follow directions.

Since texture and fertility of soil vary from garden to garden, and a wide variety of fertilizers is available from which to choose, no specific fertilization program will be discussed in this section. Instead, the *differences between the special requirements* in fertilizing will be emphasized. See the section on "Containers and Hanging Baskets," page 44, for use of fertilizer in container gardening.

The fertilization program. The first step in any fertilization program for tomatoes is to give the roots of the newly set-out plant ready access to a generous supply of phosphorus. The element phosphorus does not drain through the soil as do nitrogen and potassium. Therefore it must be placed where the newly formed roots can get to it.

The high phosphorus requirement of the plant in newly set-out garden soil may be satisfied in one of three ways:

1. Mix the fertilizer thoroughly into the soil in the area to be planted. Apply a dry fertilizer at the specified rate per foot of row (⅓ of a pound for 10 feet of row with the 5–10–10 formula), and work the fertilizer into the area to be planted.

2. Sidedress transplants with the fertilizer at the time of planting. Apply in narrow bands or furrows 3 to 4 inches away from the center of the transplant hole in a 3-inch-deep trench.

   Careless placement of the band can harm the roots or stems of the transplants if the fertilizer comes in direct contact with them. The salts in the fertilizer will draw moisture from the roots, which burns them. If the fertilizers are applied well beneath the ground, then the roots will burrow down to them and absorb the nutrients gradually. The best way to avoid fertilizer harm is to stretch a string where the row is to be planted. With a corner of a hoe, dig a furrow 3 inches deep, 3 to 4 inches to one side of, and parallel to, the string. Spread the fertilizer in the furrow and cover with soil. Repeat the banding operation on the other side of the string; then plant underneath the string.

For widely spaced plants, fertilizers can be placed in bands 6 inches long for each plant or in a circle around the plant. Run the bands 3 to 4 inches from the plant base.

3. Apply a starter solution when setting out transplants. Prepare holes large enough and deep enough to receive plants. Then fill the holes with a dilution of a high-phosphorus fertilizer (6–18–6), according to label directions and let it soak into the ground before planting.

Follow-up. Clusters of fruit call for abundant food supply. Nutrients and moisture must be constantly available for continuous leaf growth and fruit development.

When the first fruit is the size of golf balls, start your maintenance fertilization program and continue it throughout the growing season.

Watering

Frequency of watering depends upon the stage of growth of the vines, the daily temperatures, the humidity, air movement, light intensity, and the type of soil.

In one commercial planting in an area of no summer rainfall where summer temperatures average 80°F., tomatoes growing in deep clay loam are watered only twice a month.

In another planting, where rain supplies a portion of the watering needs, irrigation is scheduled on a "when needed" basis.

Commercial plantings are generally in deep soil, where the deep-rooted tomato vine finds an adequate reservoir of water. If soils are shallow or sandy, twice-a-week watering may be necessary.

If gardening is done in heavy soil, irrigation should be as infrequent as the plant will allow. The air spaces in the soil shouldn't stay filled with water.

Regardless of how watering is done, remember a sporadic water supply means trouble for the tomato plant. The most frequent cause of blossom-end rot is an uneven water supply. (See the chapter "Problems with Tomatoes," page 50.)

An effective aid in maintaining an even, continuous supply of moisture is a mulch—organic or black plastic. (See "Mulches," page 36.)

Watering should be thorough to encourage the development of a deep root system, which will help the plant withstand dry spells. Tomatoes like moisture, but overwatering is harmful. It can cause diseases and prevent new plants from setting fruit. There is no call for alarm if plants wilt on a hot summer day. They will probably recover during the night. If they don't, it's time to water.

See the section on "Containers and Hanging Baskets," page 44, for watering hints for container gardening.

Automatic watering systems. Top: This emitter is inexpensive and easy to install. Use it at the end of a spaghetti hose or install it directly into the main line. Above: A compensating emitter that releases 1 gallon per hour can maintain an even rate of flow on uneven terrain.

Below left: Ooze-system meters water to the planting area in a uniform and efficient manner.

Below middle: A filtration device (here, a simple line filter) is crucial to any drip system, because it filters out silt and algae that might otherwise clog and ruin the system.

Below: The small spaghetti-type hose works both in a hanging position and on the ground.

Mulches

Each type of mulch has a different purpose. Both clear plastic and black plastic warm the soil. They are effective *early* in the season. In cool summer areas, where an increase of soil temperature is helpful, clear plastic is used.

Black plastic, with only a moderate (several degrees) warming effect, helps stop all weed growth.

Reflective mulches—aluminum foil and mineral-coated plastic—and organic mulches are used to reduce soil temperatures and should be applied *after* the soil has warmed up.

Reflective mulches have the added benefit of increasing the light on the lower leaves that normally are shaded by the foliage above them.

Black plastic film is a favorite mulch of some gardeners. A black polyethylene mulch does a good job of keeping tomatoes off the ground, and plants mulched with it deliver yields equal to those of any type of plant training. Field tests indicate that high-quality fruit is produced when plants are allowed to sprawl naturally over the plastic. Strong-growing tomato plants should be given a space of 3 by 5 feet when grown on the plastic.

Temperature readings of the soil beneath black plastic show that the increase is generally in the range of 3° to 6°F.; sometimes only 2°. The temperature of the film itself soars high on hot sunny days and kicks back a great deal of heat to the air above it, rather than transferring it to the soil.

Black polyethylene is available in a 1- to 6-mil thickness, in rolls 3 to 6 feet wide. The 1½-mil thickness is most effective as a mulch.

A mulch of black plastic increased yields in a test planting by the University of Florida in commercial growing fields. The raised beds were 6 inches high and 48 inches wide, with 16 inches between the rows. After the beds were formed, fertilizer was mixed thoroughly into the 6-inch depth of the bed, and the beds were covered with a black plastic mulch. Two rows of tomatoes were grown on each bed. This system is also successful with cucumbers, eggplant, peppers, squash, strawberries, and other crops.

Organic mulches. In the booklet *Commercial Production of Greenhouse Tomatoes*, Agricultural Handbook No. 382, the United States Department of Agriculture (U.S.D.A.) has this to say about the mulching of greenhouse tomatoes (the same practice can be followed in applying organic mulches in the garden):

"A common practice in greenhouse tomato production is to use an organic mulch. Mulches serve the following purposes: (1) To help maintain more uniform soil moisture, thereby lessening fruit cracking; (2) to add organic matter to the soil; (3) to reduce soil compaction and thereby improve soil aeration and root growth; (4) to protect the fruit of the first cluster from touching the soil and becoming infected with soil rots; (5) to reduce the amount of spattering of water drops from the soil onto the lower leaves, thereby reducing the spread of diseases.

"A number of materials are satisfactory for mulching greenhouse tomatoes. Some of the most commonly used mulching materials are wheat straw, peanut hulls, ground corncobs, and manure. Other materials used include alfalfa, red clover, wheat and rye straw, various types of hay, sawdust, wood chips, pine needles, peat moss, rice hulls, and sugarcane bagasse.

"The choice of mulch depends on the cost and availability of the material, its ability to prevent soil compaction, its decomposition rate, its effect on the nutritional balance of the soil, its freedom from potentially harmful chemicals such as herbicides, and the possibility that it may carry a disease-producing organism into the greenhouse.

"The mulch may be applied after the soil has been sterilized and cultivated just before planting, or it may be applied after the transplants have been set in the ground beds. The mulch should be spread over the entire soil surface to a depth of 2 to 3 inches."

A black plastic mulch is easily installed before planting. Top left: Dig shallow trenches on each side of the row, spaced apart about as wide as the plastic. Then unroll the plastic along the length of the row.

Top right: Unfold the plastic evenly along the row. Secure the edges by burying them in the side trenches, then covering with soil.

Bottom left: A drip irrigation system is one convenient way to supply water underneath black plastic mulch. Install it first, then lay down the plastic.

Bottom right: When an automator is combined with black plastic mulch, watering and fertilizing is an easy task.

Black plastic. In one test garden 52 varieties of tomatoes, for a total of several hundred plants, were planted. Half of the plants were mulched with black plastic; these plants were better looking, greener, and more succulent than those handled in any other fashion. Two irrigation systems were installed. One bed was watered by the ooze system using Viaflow. The other was trickle, or drip, irrigation.

A mulch of black plastic or an organic mulch evens the water supply to the plant by reducing the water loss through evaporation. No drying out occurs in the top inch or so of soil. Loss of moisture from the leaves of the plant (transpiration) increases as the plant grows and forms additional foliage. The loss of water through transpiration of a vigorously growing vine is far greater than the loss through soil evaporation. Gear a watering schedule to the needs of the plant. The black plastic should not be expected to take care of the watering job.

In another experiment, circles of black plastic were used to cover the soil in 5-gallon nursery cans. The vines were healthier and all moisture tests favorable. With a mulch, root action takes place in the top inch of soil.

The automator. The use of the automator with a black plastic mulch (see photograph above) benefits the tomato grower in several ways:

☐ It eliminates the need for a watering system beneath the plastic.
☐ Combining it with the black plastic increases the soil area protected from weed growth and water loss through evaporation.
☐ It gives the gardener a way to add water and fertilizer, accurately and deeply, through the black plastic.

Training Tomatoes

Training begins with pruning, or pinching back (see below), which speeds up harvest but reduces yield. There are as many ways to train tomatoes as there are gardens. See, for example, pages 39 and 40.

How Many Stems?

One stem system. If getting tomatoes a couple of weeks early is important to you, training to a single stem will usually do it. Just pinch out each new stem after it has sprouted at least two leaves, as shown below.

Be aware, however, that this severe pruning will reduce your total crop greatly and also is likely to increase the incidence of blossom-end rot.

Two or more stems produce more tomatoes with better foliage protection from the sun. Choose the stems you want to keep and pinch out the others as they develop. Again, be sure to leave a couple of leaves at the base of each stem you remove.

The 4-stem plant shown here is off to a good start. But it, as well as the plant shown to the left, will need support. The following pages will show you how.

Where Should Unwanted Growth Be Pinched?

Before removing suckers or side shoots on a tomato plant, wait until two leaves develop and pinch above them. This practice provides better foliage cover to protect the fruit and stems from sun damage.

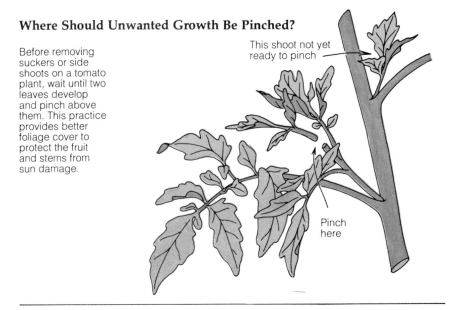

This shoot not yet ready to pinch

Pinch here

One of the oldest and most effective training methods is the simple single-stake method. Drive 8-foot-long 2 by 2s into the ground about 2 feet apart. This is for the tall-growing, indeterminate varieties. The low-growing bush-type plants should be allowed to sprawl.

Tomato transplants are planted at the base, and on the south side of each stake. As the plants grow, the sideshoots (the suckers that form at the axil of the leaf branch and the stem) are broken off. As the plant grows, the single stem, with all side branches removed, is tied at intervals to the stake.

The wire cage. The more modern method is to use a wire cage of concrete reinforcing wire or hog-wire made into a big cylinder. The mesh must be large enough to allow a reach-through for picking ripe tomatoes. Fit the cage to the plant, and let the plant grow in its own disorderly way. Anchor the cage securely so that it won't tip over in high winds.

The vine that is allowed to grow in its own disorderly fashion in a wire cage has better foliage cover and more protection against sunscald than the vine that is allowed to sprawl or is trained on a stake or trellis. The cage itself keeps the fruit off the ground, and the chores of tying and pruning are avoided.

During the first years of the training program, cages 18 inches in diameter were used. Performance and yields were satisfactory. The following season a comparison was made between performance in cages with diameters of 24 inches and 30 inches.

The 18-inch-diameter cages were satisfactory for the small, bush-type vines. However, the more vigorous and indeterminate growers showed a definite improvement in performance and yields in the 24-inch-diameter cages.

Why Use Wire Cages?

When the small bush-type tomato is allowed to sprawl, the weight of the ripening fruit opens up the bush and exposes the tomatoes to sunscald.

A small cage supports the bush-types, keeps fruit and foliage off the ground, and prevents most sunscald.

A tall cage is a very good way to support viney indeterminates or strong determinates without tying. Keep the plant pinched inside the cage until it grows up and over the top.

What Size Wire Cage?

Several years of experience in the garden, along with a recent scientific experiment (see text), have indicated the ideal size for a tomato cage. It is 24 inches in diameter and 60 inches high.

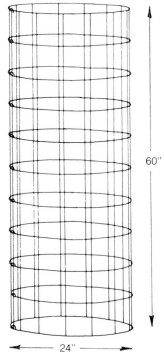

60"

24"

This size supports the vine very well, virtually prevents sunscald, and allows enough leaf surface for maximum fruiting and maximum solids in the fruit.

Other Structures for Support

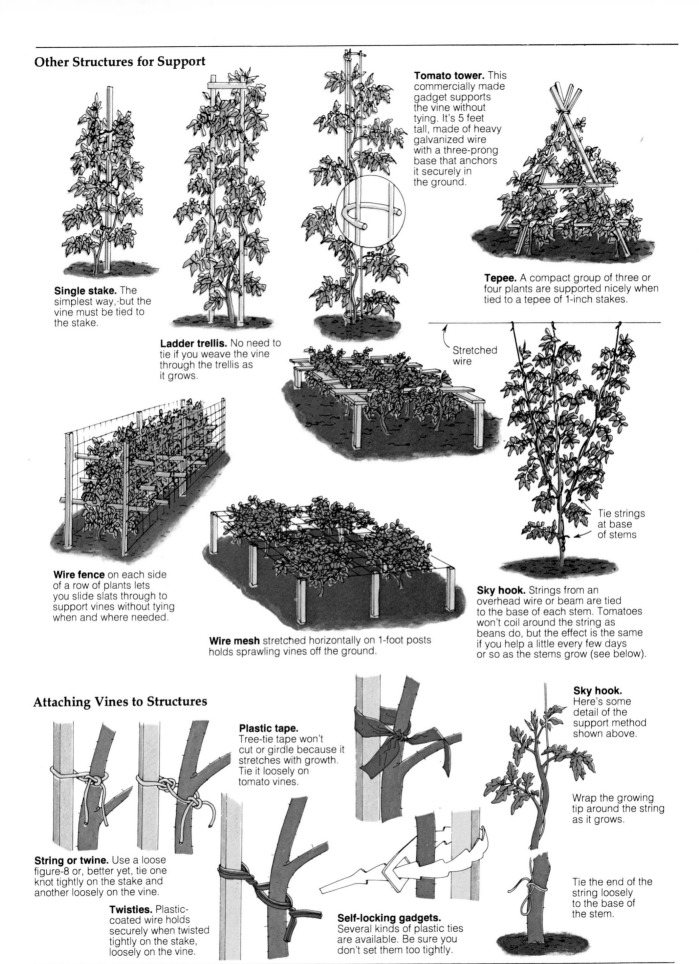

Tomato tower. This commercially made gadget supports the vine without tying. It's 5 feet tall, made of heavy galvanized wire with a three-prong base that anchors it securely in the ground.

Single stake. The simplest way, but the vine must be tied to the stake.

Ladder trellis. No need to tie if you weave the vine through the trellis as it grows.

Tepee. A compact group of three or four plants are supported nicely when tied to a tepee of 1-inch stakes.

Stretched wire

Tie strings at base of stems

Wire fence on each side of a row of plants lets you slide slats through to support vines without tying when and where needed.

Wire mesh stretched horizontally on 1-foot posts holds sprawling vines off the ground.

Sky hook. Strings from an overhead wire or beam are tied to the base of each stem. Tomatoes won't coil around the string as beans do, but the effect is the same if you help a little every few days or so as the stems grow (see below).

Attaching Vines to Structures

Sky hook. Here's some detail of the support method shown above.

Plastic tape. Tree-tie tape won't cut or girdle because it stretches with growth. Tie it loosely on tomato vines.

Wrap the growing tip around the string as it grows.

String or twine. Use a loose figure-8 or, better yet, tie one knot tightly on the stake and another loosely on the vine.

Twisties. Plastic-coated wire holds securely when twisted tightly on the stake, loosely on the vine.

Self-locking gadgets. Several kinds of plastic ties are available. Be sure you don't set them too tightly.

Tie the end of the string loosely to the base of the stem.

Greenhouse Growing

Home greenhouses are used in many ways. Their most common use is for the early starting of flowers and vegetables from seed. The greenhouse is a necessity to the hobbyist specializing in the exotic—orchids, ferns, and foliage plants, but using the greenhouse to grow vegetables in the off-season months is becoming more common.

The home gardener with an interest in growing greenhouse tomatoes commercially should realize that growing tomatoes in a greenhouse for home consumption and growing them for profit are entirely different operations.

If you are growing commercially you grow what you can sell, and what you can sell will be governed by local buying habits and ideas about what a greenhouse tomato should look like.

Dr. Victor Lambeth of Missouri University—the father of the 'Tuckcross' varieties of greenhouse tomatoes—talked about the strange pattern of regional acceptance of size and color:

"Let me give you an observation on greenhouse tomatoes as per size of fruit. The New England States want a small fruit, similar to what they grow in England. In Europe the preferred greenhouse tomatoes will not weigh over 3 or 4 ounces. But you can't get a Midwesterner to look at them.

"And there is a strong bias with respect to the skin color. There are certain areas that will accept a pink and not a red, and there are others that will accept red and not the pink. It's just like white eggs and brown eggs.

"In Canada some greenhouse growers are breaking away from the small tomato preference and breaking into the larger fruit market.

"As you go into the Deep South, winter low-light conditions improve, and you can grow the field varieties in greenhouse structures, particularly the Florida varieties like 'Tropic' and 'Manapal', and do quite well with them.

"In the West the greenhouse varieties most commonly available at supermarkets are the hydroponically grown, large-fruited 'Tropic' and 'Manapal'. They are usually identified by individual labels, as well as a difference in price."

The United Fresh Fruit and Vegetable Association sheds some light on why some stem is left on the fruit of the greenhouse tomato when harvested.

Left: Tomato plants in a greenhouse are trained to a single stem. Plastic twine provides support.

Center: These tomato vines are tied with twine at their base and the twine is stretched to an overhead wire.

Right: 'Floradel' is a successful greenhouse variety.

Left: Hot weather requires more watering—a chore if done by hand.

Center: A greenhouse lets you grow fresh vegetables throughout the year.

Right: Greenhouse tomatoes planted in winter will produce heavily in April.

"On the market, greenhouse tomatoes are judged somewhat by the freshness and greenness of their sepals, as this is an index to the length of time the fruits have been removed from the vines. Fresh sepals on full-ripe fruits indicate they were recently harvested when practically ripe. Tomatoes with stems attached lose moisture more slowly and will keep fresh for a longer time than those with stems removed."

The chapter "Tomato Varieties," pages 112 to 138, includes a list of the varieties well adapted to greenhouse growing.

Advice for the amateur. The increased interest in greenhouse growing has given the home gardener a wide choice of available greenhouse structures. It is generally agreed that the beginning greenhouse gardener should start with one of the smaller models, work with it for a season or two, and then branch out to a larger model; or, if desired, build a custom-designed unit.

The type of structure and the heating and cooling equipment required will be determined by your climate. Summer heat and winter cold are the two primary considerations.

Obviously, gardeners in mild-winter areas with a high percentage of sunlight find off-season vegetable growing far more practical than do greenhouse growers in severely cold winter areas.

To cut back on heating costs in harsh winter climates, greenhouses should be double glazed, or designed in such a way that a second layer of plastic film can be easily installed.

In areas where summers are hot, temperatures inside the greenhouse may reach levels unfavorable to blossom set. If high humidity is not a problem, an individual cooling unit, such as a "swamp cooler" or a "wet wall" unit, will bring temperatures down to an acceptable range.

The wet wall system, which has proven effective, especially in larger greenhouses, is made up of a series of wood fiber pads installed vertically on one side of the greenhouse and large exhaust fans on the other side. The exhaust fans draw air through the pads, which are kept wet by continually circulating water. The moist air coming through the pads is cooled by evaporation of the water.

If summer temperatures *and* high humidity are a problem, swamp coolers and wet wall systems will only add to the humidity problem. A refrigeration unit of some kind is recommended in these areas.

In areas where summer temperatures are not extreme, but heat build-up is still a concern—usually from May to October—temperatures can be lowered for that interim by removing the sides of the greenhouse, and replacing them with a wire screen, such as chicken wire, to keep animals out.

Growing methods. Over the years several different growing methods have been practiced by commercial greenhouse tomato growers. Home greenhouse gardeners can benefit from their experiences when choosing the method best for their own situation. Five more-or-less accepted methods have been used: bed culture, trough growing, ring culture, grow-bag culture, and hydroponic culture. Bed culture has been used for many decades, but the last four methods have been recently developed based on two principles—the use of a sterile growing medium and the confinement of the roots to a relatively small area.

Bed culture. Tomatoes are planted directly in the soil of the greenhouse floor. The enrichment of this soil with organic matter and fertilizers is much the same as with outdoor gardening. The big drawback for commercial growers, and even more of a handicap for home gardeners, is the necessity for yearly soil sterilization to control soil-borne diseases, which are particularly harmful to tomatoes.

Trough growing. Tomatoes are grown in long, narrow, plastic-lined beds, filled with a lightweight soil mix. In order to be effective, the plastic liner must be impermeable to roots. The troughs can be constructed of concrete blocks, 1 by 6 or 2 by 6-inch lumber, or similar building materials. Troughs should be 5 to 6 inches deep and about 24 inches wide to accommodate two rows of tomatoes. Drain-holes, 1 inch in diameter, should be cut on each side of the plastic liner, 1 to 2 inches from the bottom, about 10 feet apart.

Ring culture. Set a tomato plant into a round (8- to 10-inch-diameter) ring, or sleeve, of plastic film or tar paper. The rings have no top or bottom and are filled with a sterile growing medium and placed on a troughlike bed of water-absorbing, synthetic aggregate, 4 to 6 inches deep. Ring culture was originally promoted because it allows the tomato plant to form two separate root systems. It is claimed that by planting in an artificial mix (in the ring) and allowing the roots free access to the water-charged underlayer, the plants benefit from the combined advantages of soil culture and hydroculture.

Grow-bag culture. This sytem, which has been used in England for a number of years, is just beginning to appear in the United States. A plastic bag of sterile soil mix is laid flat on the greenhouse floor or bench. A cut in the top surface of the bag allows the planting of the tomato directly in the bag. The advantage is the ease of replacement of the growing medium each year.

Hydroponic culture. In this nonsoil system of growing plants, the tomatoes are grown in specially designed tanks on beds filled with aggregate or similar material. Irrigation is taken care of by an automated battery of pumps, with regularly timed nutrient applications.

Timing. As in commercial production the late spring single crop is by far the easiest greenhouse tomato crop to produce and is highly recommended for the amateur greenhouse gardener. Seeds are planted in late winter and the plants set permanently in beds in early spring. Flowering, fruit setting, and fruit growth occur during the increasingly longer and sunnier days of spring and early summer. Harvest begins much in advance of field-grown varieties, and continues until the field varieties are commonly available. Excellent crops of high-quality fruit are possible with plants producing from 8 to 12 clusters with 1 to 2 pounds of fruit per cluster.

Pruning and training. Plants, regardless of the growing method, are usually trained to a single stem. All sideshoots should be removed at least twice weekly. Plants are supported with plastic twine, one end of which is tied with a small non-slip loop to the base of the plant. The other end is attached to a wire supported 6 to 8 feet above the plant row. As the plant grows, it is twisted around the twine in one or two easy spirals for each cluster of fruit.

Above left: Two 5-gallon containers hold tomato vines trained on a one-legged A-frame.

Above right: Cherry tomatoes make edible decorations in a hanging basket.

Below: Small, determinate, bush-type tomato varieties are good candidates for container culture.

Containers and Hanging Baskets

Growing tomatoes in containers is favored by gardeners faced with two kinds of problems—unsuitable garden soil or no garden soil at all.

On balconies, decks, and paved patios container growing is the only way to create a tomato garden. Successful container growing on deck or balcony gardens depends first on the hours of sunlight the tomato plant will receive. The accepted minimum requirement is 8 hours. Trials show that the 8-hour requirement need not be met by continuous exposure, but could be fulfilled with 4 hours of sun in the morning and 4 hours in the late afternoon.

Determined container gardeners, handicapped with a difficult sun exposure, have put their containers on wheels so that the plants can be switched from one side of the balcony to the other to follow the sun.

What size container is appropriate? The minimum size depends upon how the plant's needs for a continuous supply of moisture and nutrients are met. A check of the container photographs throughout this book is the best evidence that the tomato plant will adapt itself to almost any size container.

In the chapter "Tomato Varieties," pages 112 to 138, there is a list of the tomatoes well adapted to growing in containers and hanging baskets.

Of these varieties, the favorites for use in hanging baskets are 'Small Fry' and 'Sugar Lump'. 'Small Fry' has been a consistent performer year after year. The first *ripe* fruit ripens early, and the vine continues to produce throughout the growing season.

As with all tomato plants the early growth is upright. To speed up the downward growth you may attach small weights to the branches. The weights should be about 1 ounce and made of readily available materials— nuts, bolts, lead sinkers, or steel washers.

The cultivar 'Red Cherry' is also a long-season producer in hanging baskets. High yields of small fruit are possible when it is grown indoors in late winter and early spring with plenty of light from a large window.

'Yellow Pear' is a grower too sprawling and vigorous for confinement in a hanging basket.

Synthetic soils. If you are growing tomatoes in containers, the use of a quality-controlled, synthetic soil mix is almost a must. It gives the plant the soil needed for vigorous growth and fruit production. In terms of both tomato quality and your own gardening enjoyment much can be said in favor of these lightweight "soil" mixes.

Garden stores everywhere sell special soil mixes under a wide variety of trade names: Redi-Earth, Jiffy Mix, Metro Mix, Super Soil, Pro-Mix, Baccto Potting Soil, Terra-Lite Tomato Soil, and many others.

Some mail-order seed companies package their own brands of potting soil and special tomato soils. For example, Burpee Seed Company offers its special tomato mix, Burpee Tomato Growing Formula, and Park Seed Company has its list of Sure-Fire Mixes.

Other seed companies may list their own mixes or widely distributed commercial mixes.

The basic ingredients for artificial soils. The organic portion of the mix may be peat moss, redwood sawdust, shavings, bark of hardwoods, fir bark, pine bark, or any combination of these ingredients.

Vermiculite

The mineral portion may be vermiculite, perlite, pumice, builder's sand or granite sand, or a combination of them. The most commonly used minerals are vermiculite, perlite, and fine sand.

Vermiculite (Terra-Lite) resembles mica when mined. Under heat treatment the mineral flakes expand with air spaces to twenty times their original thickness.

Perlite (sponge rock) when mined is a granitelike volcanic material that, when crushed and heat-treated at 1500° to 2000°F., pops like popcorn and expands to twenty times its original volume.

The mix you buy may be 50% peat moss and 50% vermiculite, or 50% ground bark and 50% fine sand, or other combinations of the organic and mineral components. The ingredients in the mixes vary, but the principle behind all mixes is the same—soilless "soil" must provide:

Perlite

1. Fast drainage of water through the "soil."
2. Air in the "soil" after drainage.
3. A reservoir of water in the "soil" after drainage.

Most important in any container mix is *air in the soil* after drainage. Plant roots require air for growth and respiration. In a heavy garden soil, the space between soil particles (the pore space) is small. When water is applied to the soil, it drives out air by filling the small pore spaces.

In an artificial soil mix, you have micropores and macropores (small and large pores). When the mix is irrigated, water is retained in the micropores but quickly drains through the macropores, allowing air to follow.

Container soil must have better drainage than garden soil. Water moves through a column of soil in the garden with continuous capillary action (blotter action). Break that continuity with gravel, the bottom of the container, or any other means, and water will build up where the continuity is broken. A drop of water needs another drop of water behind it to drip out of a pot or into a layer of gravel. The amount of air in the soil after drainage is the important factor in the growth of the plant.

Keep it simple. Gardeners who like to work out complicated mixes of five or six ingredients find it difficult to accept the fact that a simple combination of peat moss and vermiculite, or perlite, or fine sand, gives good results.

The quality soil mixes are ready to use as is. Fill the container (5-gallon size or larger) with the mix, set the transplant in it, and watch it grow.

In 5-gallon containers, with a large vine trained on sticks or tomato towers, you may prefer a mix slightly heavier than the mix that comes in the bag. Don't assume that the mix can't be tampered with. The addition of sand (10% by volume) will merely add to the weight of the mix. The mix will still be free from disease-causing organisms, insects, and weed seeds. With sand added, the container will be heavy enough to prevent vine and can from toppling over in the wind.

Buy a 2-cubic-foot bag and you have enough "soil" for four 5-gallon-size containers.

Remember that when growing tomatoes in containers, the smaller the container the more frequently you must water and fertilize. Frequent watering leaches nitrogen and potassium through the soil mix in the container—which may seem like a waste of fertilizer, but when water leaches elements through the soil it also prevents a build-up of the harmful salt contents of the mix. Salts in the irrigation water are leached through the soil. When watering plants in containers, continue watering until the water drains out of the container.

The amount of nutrients required daily is very small. But the supply must be continuous. When frequent waterings are needed in hot weather, the leaching action of the water drains away a part of the nutrient supply. That's why experienced container gardeners adjust their fertilization program to the watering schedule rather than to the calendar. To them, continuous feeding with a weak nutrient solution is ideal.

Container fertilization. Commercial synthetic soil mixes usually contain the necessary phosphorus for good plant growth.

Start a regular fertilization program two to three weeks after setting out transplants and continue it throughout the growing season.

Remember, the restricted root space and the frequent watering calls for more applications of fertilizer than when the tomato plant is garden grown.

Container watering. Watering a 4-foot-high tomato plant in a 6-inch-deep box by hand is practical if you are home during the growing season and enjoy watering. If hand-watering becomes a chore, set up a multiple-container watering system with one of the drip irrigation units.

Important: Whether tomatoes are being grown in containers or in garden soil, the objective in watering is to provide a continuous supply of moisture. Keep the following points in mind:

☐ When filling containers with soil, be sure to leave enough room at the top for water: 2 inches for the standard 5-gallon container; 3 inches for a 10-gallon container.
☐ Water the container thoroughly—until the water runs out the drainage hole.
☐ Root rot caused by overly wet soil can be prevented by not placing containers in saucers where the water accumulates.

Experiments

With deck, balcony, and patio gardeners in mind, experiments were made to determine answers to some frequently asked questions about growing tomatoes in containers:

☐ Is a special soil mix necessary?
☐ What size container is best?
☐ How can vines be trained?

The effect of container size on yield and plant growth is detailed below.

Container soil-mix test. Soil mixes were tested in a Los Angeles test garden. The objective of the test was to compare the locally available top soil to quality-controlled synthetic soil mixes.

The tomato cultivar chosen for the test was 'Better Boy'. Transplants were purchased at a local nursery and planted out on April 20 in a series of six

The same variety—'Better Boy'—growing in three different sizes of containers: The container at left holds 4 cubic feet of soil; the middle box holds 2 cubic feet; and the can on the right holds ½ cubic foot. As you can see, the largest container produced the biggest plant, but it was the smallest container at right that produced the biggest yield of fruit.

containers, each 24 inches square by 12 inches deep. Four of the containers were filled with topsoil. The other two containers were filled with synthetic soil mix.

The fertilizing, mulching, and watering program was the same for all plants throughout the experiment.

Results. The tomatoes grown in topsoil showed water stress, but fruited and ripened earlier. The plants grown in synthetic soil produced twice as much fruit per plant.

Container size test. The minimum volume of soil required to grow a quality crop of tomatoes in containers has long been debated. In this experiment three quantities of standard soil mix—4 cubic feet, 2 cubic feet, and ½ cubic foot—were tried.

'Better Boy' tomatoes were planted in three different sized containers in the same soil mix on the same day.

All were watered and fertilized in the same way. Only the soil volume varied.

45 days after planting. The plants in the three containers were compared 45 days after planting. All the plants were thriving—with green leaves, flowers, and actually some fruit set. The major difference among them was in the height of the plants. The tomato plants in ½-cubic-foot containers were definitely smaller.

90 days after planting. After another six weeks the plants were measured again. Again, all the plants showed good vigor, strong new growth, and continued fruit set. This time, however, the difference among the three soil volumes showed in both height of plant and the load of ripening fruit.

The chart clearly shows that the larger the volume of soil, the larger the tomato harvest. But if you're talking about maximum production from the minimum amount of soil, bear in mind that a 4-cubic-foot container holds enough soil to fill eight 5-gallon containers. If you have the deck space for eight 5-gallon containers, the total yield from those eight plants will be almost double that of the plants in the 4-cubic-foot box.

Container Soil-Mix Test

	Top soil	Synthetic soil mix
Days to flower	20	20
Days to set fruit	42	49
Days to ripe fruit	84	94
Lbs. of ripe fruit @ 98 days	4.5	9.0

Soil Volume

45 days			
Soil volume	4 cu. ft.	2cu. ft.	½ cu. ft.
Height	30"	27"	21"

90 days			
Soil volume	4 cu. ft.	2 cu. ft.	½ cu. ft.
Height	66"	56"	46"
Fruit	58	48	12

A lath trellis supports productive vines of 'Vineripe', 'Tropic', and 'Springset'. All grow in ½ cubic foot of soil in 5-gallon nursery cans. A short wooden screen hides the cans from view.

Trellis training. An experiment was conducted to measure production from a container filled with ½ cubic foot of soil mix, the equivalent of a 5-gallon can. The *only* difference between this experiment and the last one was the training method. The cultivars 'Big Set', 'Vineripe', 'Springset', and 'Tropic' were all trained on either a wire or lath trellis. Pruning was kept to a bare minimum, all shoots being tied to the trellis.

One slight variable was that 'Vineripe', 'Springset', and 'Tropic' were planted in 5-gallon nursery cans, whereas 'Big Set' was grown in wooden boxes 12 inches square by 8 inches deep.

45 days after planting. The plants showed good growth, flowers, and fruit set. The first two flower clusters had set fruit, and the clusters were full.

90 days after planting. The plants were vigorously growing. Flowers were blooming on the new growth, young fruits were setting, and the lower leaves were still a rich green color. The best performer of the four varieties had 31 ripening fruits; the lowest had 25. The average was 29 fruits per plant. Three dozen ripe tomatoes had already been picked and more were appearing.

Other training notes. A tomato's performance in a 5-gallon container is strongly influenced by the training method. In the 'Better Boy' experiment, where the 5-gallon container is compared to the larger-size containers, the tomato was pruned and trained on a tomato tower. (See photo, page 47). This method produced larger and earlier fruit than the plants in the larger containers. However, in all tests of production in 5-gallon containers, the number of fruits is greater when the vine is trained in a fan shape, on a trellis of wire or wood.

What advantage does deep planting offer? The general rule in transplanting is "never plant deeper than it grew in the nursery." The tomato plant has the ability to develop roots along the stem, wherever the stem comes in contact with moist soil. For that reason set any tomato transplant deep in the soil—up to its first leaves.

To find the difference in growth of the deep-planted tomato and the one planted normally, one cultivar was planted in both ways. The results are shown in the photographs on page 49.

Are the experiments valid? Can the experiments be repeated in another garden situation with comparable results? A description of the control factors in the final two experiments and the climatic conditions of the experiment follows.

Training Method

	# Fruit at 90 days
'Big Set'	31
'Springset'	32
'Vineripe'	25
'Tropic'	29
Average	29

Roots of deeply planted transplants form in two places—from the rootball and all along the buried stem. Left: A transplant 30 days after deep planting. Right: Another transplant, also 30 days after planting, but planted at the same depth at which it grew in the nursery.

Special soil mix. The soil mix was made up of 45% sphagnum peat moss, 45% perlite, and 10% sand. To 1 cubic yard of this mix these fertilizers and amendments were added:

☐ 8 lbs of 5–10–10 fertilizer
☐ 10 lbs. of agricultural lime

Any of the quality-controlled commercial mixes such as Jiffy Mix, Redi-Earth, or Super-Soil will give you equal, if not better results.

Temperature and sunlight. Sunlight and daily temperature will, of course, vary from garden to garden. Under ideal circumstances, every tomato plant used in any of the experiments would have the same amount of sunlight. They didn't.

Some got the morning sun, some the afternoon sun. Some vines that received 7 hours of sunlight in June were in shade most of the day in late September.

As with all gardens everywhere, the sunny spots become fewer as the garden grows older. The shade tree spreads wider and wider. The neighbor's hedge blocks the late afternoon sun.

Does the amount of sunlight affect performance? The vines in the 5-gallon containers with a trellis receiving 7 hours sun gave more ripe fruit than the vines in the 5-gallon containers in the shady locations, but both were heavy with fruit.

In sun or partial sun the vines produced a satisfactory number of ripe tomatoes.

The temperatures were generally in the mid 70s and low 80s. As always, temperatures varied widely; during this experiment an early heat wave hit when the container tomatoes were about 18 inches high.

For six days the temperature exceeded 97°F.; on four of those days it reached 102°. Until this time, the tomatoes had been growing well in the early spring weather, but how would they stand the sudden twenty- to thirty-degree jump in temperature?

The plants were watered liberally; the containers were filled until water ran out the drainage holes. This increased watering got the plants through the heat wave, but it was the porous soil mix that allowed the frequent watering, without fear of waterlogging the roots of the plants.

The tomatoes withstood the heat without wilt. That week's flowers failed to set fruit, but when the temperatures returned to the mid 70s the normal fruit set resumed.

Some of the problems you may have to
contend with (clockwise from top left) are:
hornworms; whiteflies; bacterial spot; and
damage caused by spider mites.

PROBLEMS WITH TOMATOES

Many disease-resistant varieties have been developed, but problems and troubles still occur, which can often be handled by diagnosis and treatment as explained here.

Plant breeders and researchers specializing in tomatoes have isolated many of the particular characteristics of the tomato and have discovered the location of the gene or genes responsible for that characteristic on individual chromosomes. The chromosome map on page 52 shows the inner workings of the tomato. You don't have to understand the map to know that it spells help to gardeners who have had trouble growing tomatoes, especially trouble with diseases.

Tomatoes with increased disease resistance and wider adaptation are being developed as more characteristics are mapped, or located on the tomato's chromosomes. At this time it is possible to breed into a single variety resistance to, or tolerance of, 15 different diseases and disorders.

Not yet on the genetic map, but a very important characteristic in breeding lines, is resistance to verticillium wilt and fusarium wilt—two of the most troublesome diseases of tomatoes.

Physiological Disorders: "V," "F," and "N"

The best way to avoid problems due to verticillium wilt, fusarium wilt, and nematodes is to plant disease-resistant varieties.

The resistance to disease is a part of the name of many varieties; for example: 'Wonder Boy VFN', 'Jet Star VF', and 'Burpee VF'. ("V," "F," and "N" are the initials to look for when choosing varieties, if you've had trouble with these diseases or nematodes in the past.)

Fusarium and verticillium wilts are diseases caused by fungus infections and may occur in the same soil. At times they are hard to distinguish from one another. The progress of verticillium wilt is speeded by temperatures of 70° to 75°F. and retarded by the higher temperatures that are most favorable to fusarium wilt.

A plant infected with verticillium wilt can still produce tomatoes, but fusarium wilt is more serious and wipes out the entire crop.

Verticillium wilt. The first symptom is yellowing of the older leaves, accompanied by a slight wilting of the tips of the shoots during the day. The older yellowed leaves gradually wither and drop, and eventually the crown of the plant is defoliated. The leaves higher up the stem become dull looking, and the leaflets tend to curl upward.

All branches are uniformly affected and have a tendency to be less erect than those of healthy plants. The plants usually live through the season but are somewhat stunted, and the fruits are small. In late stages of the disease, only the leaves near the tips of the branches remain alive. The loss of the lower leaves and the stunting of the later growth expose the fruit to the sun, and much of the crop is often lost because of sunscald.

Fusarium wilt. According to U.S.D.A. studies, fusarium wilt is one of the most prevalent and damaging diseases of tomatoes in many of the tomato-

Chromosome Map of Tomato

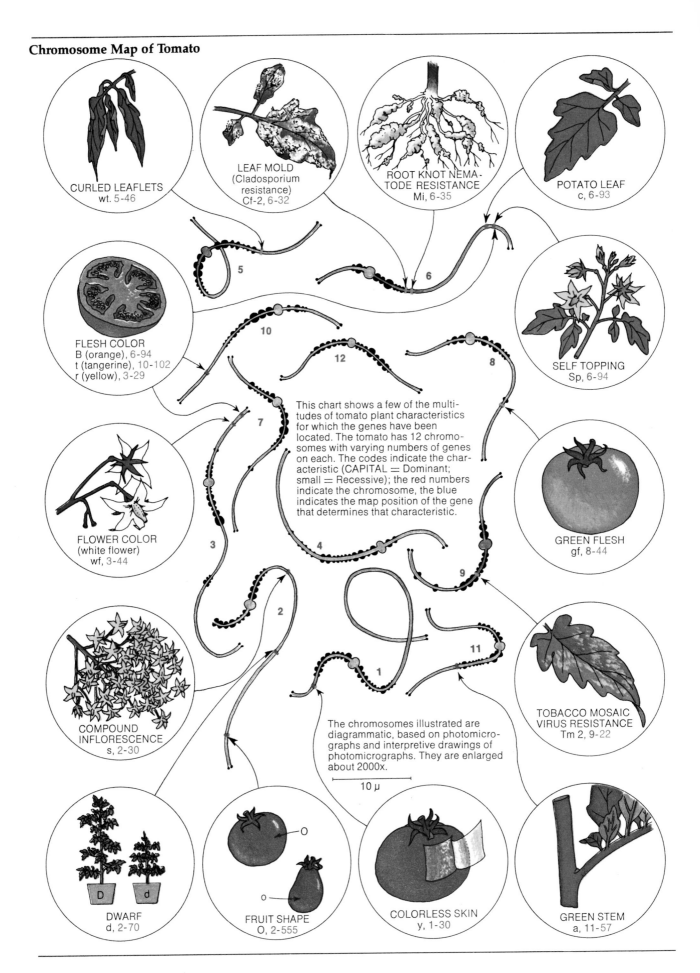

CURLED LEAFLETS
wt, 5-46

LEAF MOLD
(Cladosporium
resistance)
Cf-2, 6-32

ROOT KNOT NEMA-
TODE RESISTANCE
Mi, 6-35

POTATO LEAF
c, 6-93

5

6

FLESH COLOR
B (orange), 6-94
t (tangerine), 10-102
r (yellow), 3-29

10

12

8

SELF TOPPING
Sp, 6-94

7

This chart shows a few of the multi-
tudes of tomato plant characteristics
for which the genes have been
located. The tomato has 12 chromosomes with varying numbers of genes
on each. The codes indicate the characteristic (CAPITAL = Dominant;
small = Recessive); the red numbers
indicate the chromosome, the blue
indicates the map position of the gene
that determines that characteristic.

FLOWER COLOR
(white flower)
wf, 3-44

3

4

GREEN FLESH
gf, 8-44

2

9

COMPOUND
INFLORESCENCE
s, 2-30

11

TOBACCO MOSAIC
VIRUS RESISTANCE
Tm 2, 9-22

1

The chromosomes illustrated are
diagrammatic, based on photomicrographs and interpretive drawings of
photomicrographs. They are enlarged
about 2000x.

10 μ

DWARF
d, 2-70

O
o
FRUIT SHAPE
O, 2-555

COLORLESS SKIN
y, 1-30

GREEN STEM
a, 11-57

growing regions of the United States. The fungus is soil-borne, found in both field and greenhouse soils. The organism generally does not cause serious losses unless soil and air temperature are rather high (80° to 90°F.) during much of the season. Where such conditions prevail, plants of susceptible varieties either are killed or severely damaged when grown in infested soil.

In seedling plants, fusarium wilt causes drooping and downward curvature of the oldest leaves, usually followed by wilting and death of the plant. Older plants in the field are infected at all stages of growth, but the disease generally becomes most evident when the fruit is beginning to mature. The earliest symptom is yellowing of the lower leaves. Often some of the leaves on only one side of the stem turn yellow at first; also the leaflets on one side of the petiole may be affected before the others. The yellowed leaves gradually wilt and die and, as the disease progresses, yellowing and wilting continue up the stem until eventually all the foliage is killed and the stem dies.

Frequently a single shoot is killed before the rest of the plant shows much injury. The stem of a wilted plant shows no soft decay, but if it is cut lengthwise, the woody part next to the green outer cortex shows a dark brown discoloration of the water-conducting tissues.

Nematodes. Tiny parasitic eelworms called nematodes cause severe damage to tomato plants. Their presence should be suspected when poor stands, stunted plants, wilting of some plants more than others, and plant death are noticed. Plant injury can be found by examining the roots for swollen, knotty galls (see illustration on page 55) or brown, sheared-off areas.

Controlling nematodes is practical and inexpensive using the in-the-row fumigation method. Open a trench 6 inches deep where tomatoes are to be planted. Dribble in the fumigant at the manufacturer's recommended rate. Fill the trench immediately, and wet the surface with water to seal the fumigant in the soil. Allow sufficient time before planting for proper aeration. Read and follow all label directions.

Among the products the University of Florida recommends for fumigating soil prior to planting are: Dowfume W-85, Soilbrom 85, Vidden D, Fumazine 86E, Nemagon 50%, Nemagon 12EC, Oxy BBC 12E, Vapam, VPM, and Vorlex.

Specialists at the University of Florida also state: "Where nematode injury is suspected after tomato plants are up and growing, Nemagon (granules or liquid) may be applied to the root zone. However, such post-transplanting applications may cause injury to the plants and should be made only as a last resort."

Other Physiological Disorders

Besides the triple threat of "V," "F," and "N," many more problems can plague the tomato.

Stress. High temperatures will put the tomato plant under *stress* not only in water deficiency but in the normal coloring process.

Prevention means going back to the fundamentals: Give the plant what it needs—a constant supply of moisture, and a constant supply of nutrients. When a plant is *stressed* for water and then heavily watered, you can expect blossom-end rot.

Blossom-end rot. Symptoms of this disease appear as a leathery scar or rot on the blossom end of fruits. Blossom-end rot can occur at any stage of development. It is usually caused by sudden changes in soil moisture. It is most serious when plants growing rapidly with high soil moisture are hit by a hot (temperatures above 90°F.), dry spell. Lack of calcium in the plant is another cause of blossom-end rot. (See page 32 for how to add calcium to soil.)

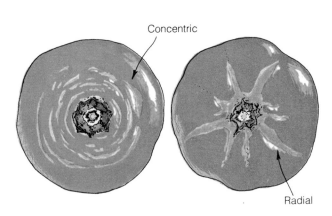

Concentric

Radial

Growth Cracks

Blossom-end Rot

Catface

Mulch plants with black plastic or organic material to reduce fluctuations in soil moisture and temperature. Do not plant in poorly drained soil.

Staked and heavily pruned tomatoes seem more susceptible to blossom-end rot than plants trained without pruning.

Blossom drop. This frustrating habit of the tomato plant is discussed in detail on pages 19 and 20. Throughout the presentation of cultivars (pages 112 to 138), those varieties with the ability to set fruit under adverse conditions are noted.

Tomato gardeners have worked out many ways to increase blossom set. These have been successful:

☐ In early spring, increase night temperatures by covering the young plants with plastic tents or similar coverings. (See page 33.)
☐ Use windbreaks to protect the plants from strong winds.
☐ Vibrate the individual flower clusters daily to increase fertilization or use special plant hormone sprays on early flowers. (See pages 20 and 21.)

Catfacing. Cool and cloudy weather at the time of flowering may cause the blossom to stick to the small fruits, resulting in the malformation of the fruits as they develop. The blossom ends of fruit are puckered, with scars between the lumps. Deep cavities may penetrate the fruit.

Catfacing occurs most frequently on early harvest fruits, usually on the large-fruited cultivars.

The best control is to plant varieties resistant to catfacing. (See pages 112 to 138.)

Fruit cracks. Fruit cracks are of two distinct types—radial and concentric (see illustration). Radial cracking is the commonest and results in the greatest fruit damage. It occurs most often during rainy periods when the temperature is relatively high (above 90°F.), especially when rains follow a long dry period—conditions which promote extremely rapid growth. Radial cracking is severest on ripening and full-ripe fruits. Tomatoes exposed to the sun develop more cracks than those well covered with foliage.

The use of crack-resistant cultivars, maintaining a uniform water supply through the use of irrigation or mulches, and keeping a good foliage cover will help reduce cracking. (See pages 112 to 138 for crack-resistant cultivars.)

Sunscald

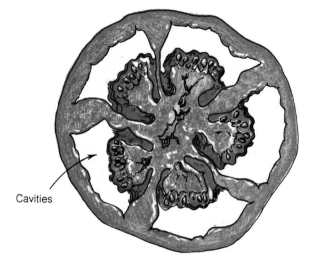

Cavities

Puffiness

Leaf roll. The leaf roll discussed in this section is not the leaf roll caused by pests or disease. This type of leaf roll is caused by prolonged rains adding too much moisture to the soil, or by severe pruning. Some tomato cultivars are more inclined to roll than others.

Lower leaves are the first to roll. The rolling continues up the plant. Leaflets may cup and overlap. Leaves feel firm and leathery.

The best control is to maintain a uniform soil moisture—by using a plastic mulch and irrigating regularly.

Misshapen fruit. Tomato gardeners are well acquainted with abnormal or misshapen fruits. Bulges and knots sometimes appear on varieties that should be round and smooth.

Young plants exposed to temperatures of 55°F. or lower will usually produce rough or misshapen fruit on the first cluster. Such low temperatures interfere with the growth of pollen tubes and normal fertilization of the ovary.

The most common abnormalities are pointed fruit with an elongated blossom end, or puffy fruit in which air spaces have developed.

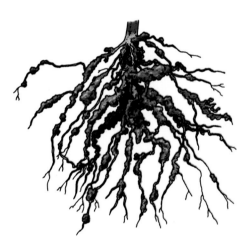

Root-knot Nematodes

Puffiness. In extreme cases a "puffy" tomato resembles a bell pepper, having normal outer walls and a hollow inside.

Puffiness appears most frequently in early harvests. It is caused by any condition that interferes with normal pollination—temperatures above 90°F. or below 55°F., low light, excessive nitrogen, or heavy rainfall, particularly when accompanied by low temperatures. It can also be caused by chemical sprays intended to increase early yields. No reliable controls have been found.

Sunscald. The U.S.D.A. has this to say about sunscald: "Sunscald is most common on immature, green fruit. At first a yellow or white patch appears on the side of the fruit toward the sun. This spot may merely remain yellow as the fruit ripens, but frequently the tissues are more severely damaged and a blisterlike area develops. Later this shrinks and forms a large, flattened, grayish-white spot with a dry paperlike surface."

Cultivars differ in resistance to sunscald. Those with poor foliage cover, or cultivars susceptible to sunscald damage, can be grown in cages rather than allowed to sprawl and expose their fruits to the sun.

5× life size   Flea beetle

Anthracnose

Early blight

Tomato fruitworm

Late blight

Gray leaf spot

Tobacco mosaic

Aphids

Insect Troubles

The actual damage done by insects to tomato plants and fruits is minimal compared to the damage they do by spreading diseases from plant to plant. It is for this latter reason that control of insects is important. Also recommended is the removal of weeds from areas where tomatoes are grown; they are breeding and hiding places for many insects. See the chart and illustrations on these pages for more information about insects and diseases to which tomatoes are susceptible.

Whiteflies. No pest can be as frustrating as whiteflies. They usually appear in clusters rather than individually. Disturb a leaf on which they are feeding and they fly away in a cloud of small white wings.

Both adults and larvae damage plants by sucking sap from foliage and excreting sticky honeydew, which coats foliage and fruits. A black sooty fungus then grows on the honeydew, giving the plants an unsightly appearance. Heavy whitefly infestation can cause wilting and death of foliage. Adult whiteflies mate, and females begin laying eggs within 2 days after emerging from the larval stage. Each female lays 100 or more eggs, generally on the underside of leaves, at the rate of 13 to 17 a day.

Under normal temperatures, 30 to 36 days are required for development from egg to adult. Once a whitefly infestation becomes established on a crop, all stages will be present. None of the insecticides available for use is effective in controlling all of the life stages. Most materials will control adults and one or more immature stages, but other stages will continue to develop. For this reason, repeated applications are necessary.

Timing and frequency of insecticide applications are the most important part of controlling whiteflies. U.S.D.A. research found that an application of Malathion four times at 10-day intervals reduced whitefly numbers 26.5%, while the same material applied eight times at 5-day intervals caused a 99.7% reduction. Make sure that the product used is approved for use on tomatoes according to the label. Make sure plants receive thorough coverage when being sprayed, and, of course, the product label instructions should be read carefully.

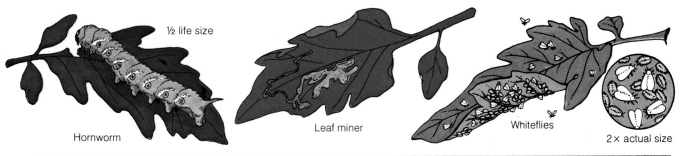

½ life size

Hornworm

Leaf miner

Whiteflies

2× actual size

Insects and Diseases

Pest or disease	Symptoms	Control
Aphids (plant lice) Attack plants from the seedling stage, through the growing season.	Suck sap; weaken the plant. May deform and stunt the infected terminals and fruit. Honey dew secretions attract fungus.	Spray with Malathion or Diazinon. Follow instructions on label.
1) **Blister beetles** May attack foliage during midsummer. 2) **Flea beetles** Attack the foliage of young plants until first fruit set. 3) **Colorado potato beetle** General feeder throughout the growing season.	1) Rarely destroy significant amount of foliage. Severe irritation or blistering may occur if beetles are crushed and come into contact with skin. 2) Leaves look as if they had been shot through with tiny holes. 3) Humpbacked larvae hatch; chew on leaves.	1) When harvesting fruit, be careful how you remove Blister beetles—don't crush them. Spray or dust with Sevin. 2) Spray or dust with Sevin. Repeat as directed. Also Diazinon spray products. 3) Spray or dust with Sevin when damage is first noticed.
Cutworms Most destructive to early season plantings.	Hide in soil during the day, feed at night. Cut off young transplants near the soil surface.	Clean them out of the soil before planting with a soil application of Diazinon dust.
Hornworms Generally seen on mature foliage.	Eat leaves and fruit, leaving only midribs.	Handpicking is successful for a few plants, or control with Sevin or Diazinon.
Leafhoppers Damage throughout the season.	Leafhoppers suck the sap from the leaves, causing curling and brown margins on the leaves.	Spray or dust with Malathion or Sevin. Follow label instructions.
Leafminers Seldom a serious problem. Can occur at any time.	Larvae make long, slender, winding white tunnels in the leaves which may result in leaf loss. Tunnels provide entrance sites for diseases.	Spray with Diazinon. Apply as directed.
Tomato fruitworm A pest the whole season long.	Eats into the fruits.	Control difficult after worms are ½-inch long. Control worms when they are small with Sevin.
Early blight Cause: *Alternaria solani*, a fungus. A problem in moist areas of spring and summer rain. First noticed on leaves, and on fruit as it matures. Not a problem in the arid West.	Small, irregular brown, dead spots appear on lower, older leaves. Spots enlarge to ½-inch in diameter in "bull's-eye" patterns. Leaf tissue around spots yellows. With severe spotting, entire leaf may yellow. Greatest injury occurs as fruit begins to mature. Older fruits may show dark, leathery, sunken spots, which may be large, and in "bull's-eye" markings. Dark dry decay may extend deep into fruit.	Spray or dust plants every 7 to 10 days with Chlorothalonil, Maneb, Zineb, or Captan. Repeat after rains to keep plants protected.
Bacterial spot Cause: *Xanthomonas vesicatoria*, a bacteria.	Small, water-soaked spots enclosing black pustules appear on fruits. Spots sink; scabs form. Infected flower stems cause blossom drop. Seedling stems may be spotted. On mature plants the older leaves are mainly affected. Leaves show irregular dark, greasy spots. Spot centers dry out and tear. Defoliation may be severe.	Use commercial disease-free seed.
Late blight Cause: *Phytophthora infestans*, a fungus. Can be serious during long periods of muggy weather with cool nights and moderately warm days. Hot dry weather checks the advance of the fungus.	Greasy, black areas on leaf margins, spreading over the whole leaf. Fine gray mold on underside of leaf during wet periods. Green and ripe fruits get corky brown on surfaces, develop an "orange peel" texture.	Spray or dust plants every 7 to 10 days with Chlorothalonil, Maneb, Zineb, or Captan. Repeat after rains to keep plants protected.
Anthracnose Cause: *Collecotrichum phoimoides*, a fungus. Appears during high August temperatures with heavy rains or dews. More prevalent in poorly drained soils.	Attacks fruit and sometimes foliage. Infected fruit have sunken, circular, water-soaked spots. Spots get deeper and larger, with blackish centers. Entire fruit rots. Oldest leaves are most vulnerable. Yellow areas surround dead spots.	Chlorothalonil, Captan, and Maneb control this disease. Follow dusting program on product labels.
Curly top virus Virus is carried by the sugar beet leafhopper. Is a big problem in central and eastern Oregon and the Willamette Valley.	Plant is stunted and yellowish. Foliage is rolled and twisted, stiff and leathery. Severe root loss. Plant may die.	Check the new curly top resistant varieties. Control insects with Sevin dust.

THE TOMATO'S RELATIVES

A little-known fact about the tomato is the extent of its family. Varieties of peppers and potatoes, the eggplant, and other unexpected plants are all related.

The tomato is a member of the nightshade family (Solanaceae), a surprisingly varied group that includes several notoriously poisonous plants, plus such well-known flowers as the petunia, nicotiana, browallia, nierembergia, schizanthus, and other major sources of garden color. It also embraces several popular vegetables that have an important place in the modern garden. The family comprises herbs, shrubs, and trees with alternate leaves, fruits that are berries, and flowers that usually have their parts in groups of five.

Peppers

The pepper (*Capsicum* species) is as temperamental as the tomato. It requires plenty of warm weather but in extremely high summer heat will not set fruit. Blossom drop can be expected when day temperatures reach 90°F. As with tomatoes, *night* temperature is also important. Fruit setting is poor when night temperatures are below 55° or above 75°F. Plants should not be set out until weather is consistently warm. Early planting followed by cool weather stunts growth, from which the plants never fully recover.

Growing zones. The hot valleys of New Mexico, Arizona, and California are ideal pepper country. In Oregon's Willamette Valley, the early varieties and the standard sweet bell peppers perform best. In the East and Midwest, plant peppers in the warmest and sunniest part of the garden. Where the harvest season is cut short by frost, green peppers can be stored in a cool, dry place for several weeks.

The decorative peppers. Many of the peppers lead a double life—as vegetables, and as glamorous ornamentals in the flower border or as container plants (in tubs, boxes, or large pots). Their beauty in flower, foliage, and fruit earns them a place in the garden or on the patio, even if a pepper is never eaten.

Peppers are of many types and numerous cultivars. The sweet-fleshed, big bells—ideally suited for stuffing—are represented by 'Bell Boy', 'California Wonder', 'Yolo Wonder', and 'Early Calwonder'. In the cooler Northwest, recommended varieties are: 'Yolo Wonder', 'Midway', 'Early Calwonder', and 'Canape Hybrid'. All of these are generally harvested in their crisp, green stage, but all turn red at maturity. Bell peppers that remain yellow when fully ripe are 'Golden Calwonder' and 'Golden Bell'.

All sweet peppers are not bell peppers. For example, the variety 'Sweet Banana', with its long, yellow, slender fruit is great for salads or frying. 'Italian Sweet' is an early green pepper.

The heart-shaped pimiento is highly ornamental as a container plant, and the fruit is usually allowed to ripen into a deep red.

Those who know their peppers advise that the garden should give space to the moderately hot 'Anaheim Chili'. When this pepper is boiled,

A few of the many cultivars of peppers: 'Hungarian Yellow Wax', 'Serrano Chile', 'Santa Fe Grande', 'Anaheim', 'Jalapeno', and 'Mercury Floral Gem'.

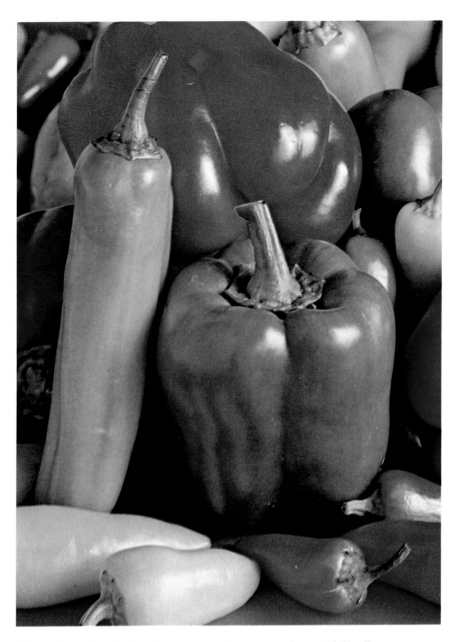

skinned, and stuffed with meat or cheese, you have *Chili rellenos*, a tasty Mexican dish.

Some of the most attractive plants grown in containers have been these hot peppers: 'Sweet Banana', like its namesake in color and shape, is yellow at first and then turns bright red when ripe; the small, hot 'Tabasco', first yellow then red, upright on the plant; the long, thin, twisted 'Cayenne', which hangs like Christmas tree ornaments.

In cooler climates the hot peppers to try are: 'Hungarian Wax', with its long yellow fruit; 'Red Cherry', with small, round fruit held upright on strong 20-inch-high plants; and 'Long Thin Cayenne', a very hot pepper.

Eggplant

Don't try to rush the season with eggplant (*Solanum melongena*). Set out plants only after the weather has warmed up—when daytime temperatures are in the 70°F. range. The plant is more susceptible to cold damage than the tomato. You'll get a higher quality fruit when development is rapid and uninterrupted.

Try the new Oriental varieties. They're smaller than the eggplants you see in the supermarket, but they require less heat for production.

Container planting. Eggplant makes an attractive container plant and does very well in a 5-gallon can or box. Place the container in one of the warmer spots in your garden for the best results.

Harvesting the immature fruit. Eggplant should be used just after harvest as a *fresh* vegetable, not held in storage. For best eating quality, harvest while it is immature and the flesh is firm. In mature fruits the seeds become brown, the seed coats harden, and the flesh softens.

Since you can't see inside the fruits to check the stage of development, it's difficult to tell when they're just right. Harvest the fruits regularly as they reach a usable size.

Harvest oval varieties when they are 4 to 6 inches long and 3 to 4 inches wide; slim types, when they are 5 to 6 inches long and 2 to 3 inches in diameter. When all fruits are harvested at the immature stage, plants usually set more fruits than when some are allowed to go to full maturity.

Ten days following harvest should be the maximum time for storing the fruits before they lose moisture, shrivel, and get flabby. Keep them in a plastic bag to retard moisture loss. Eggplant is subject to chilling injury at temperatures lower than 50°F. Store in a cool place rather than in the refrigerator.

Top left: Eggplants require secure staking to support the heavy fruit.
Top right: Japanese eggplant.
Above: Husk tomatoes.

Husk Tomato

The husk tomato (*Physalis peruviana*) is a perennial, listed in seed catalogs as 'Ground Cherry' and 'Poha Berry'. The ornamental Chinese-lantern plant (*P. alkekengi*) is a close relative. The plant grows from 1½ to 2½ feet tall with oval or heart-shaped fuzzy leaves growing in pairs on the stem. The fruits, about the same size as the cherry tomato, are produced inside a paperlike husk. When ripe, the husks turn brown and the fruits drop from the plant. If left in the husks, they will keep for several weeks.

The husk tomato has a pleasing and distinctive flavor and is used raw in cocktails or for a dessert. It is frequently used in pies or as a cooked sauce on cakes and puddings, but the most popular way of using pohas is in jam.

Tomatillo

The tomatillo (*Physalis ixocarpa*) is an annual, growing 3 to 4 feet high. Leaves are long, oval shaped, and deeply notched. Fruit is smooth and sticky, either green or purplish in color, and entirely enclosed in a thin husk. Fruit is 1 to 2 inches in diameter, growing to about the size and shape of a walnut.

Top right: Inside its husk, the tomatillo is solid-fleshed.

Bottom right: The tomatillo is similar in appearance to its close relative, the husk tomato.

A close relative of the husk tomato or ground cherry, the tomatillo has a flavor that is tart, rather than sweet like the husk tomato, tasting somewhat like green apples.

It can be used in many ways in Mexican cooking. Raw or cooked, it gives sauces a rich, distinctive flavor. It is used fresh in salads, in tacos, and in sandwiches.

Grow tomatillos in the same way as tomatoes. Seed that is sown in peat pots will germinate in about 5 days and be ready to transplant in 2 to 3 weeks.

Tomatillos are harvested according to use. For highest-quality fruit, harvest fresh when the husks change color from green to tan. For cooking, harvest at any time. Left on the vine, they become yellow and mild.

Tomatillos can be stored for months. Some gardeners store the fruit on the vine; some spread out the picked fruit, still in the husks, in a cool place with good air circulation.

Irish Potatoes

Measured in pounds or dollar return per square foot of garden space, potatoes (*Solanum tuberosum*) deserve a place in the smallest garden.

You can start new plants from the potatoes you buy at the market. However, market potatoes might carry plant disease and might have been treated to prevent sprouting. In any case, freshly dug potatoes won't sprout until they have had a rest period.

It's best to start with certified seed potatoes, or seed pieces, or "eyes" from garden stores and mail-order seed companies. Good-size seed pieces increase the chances for a good yield. Cut pieces about 1½ inches square, making sure that at least one good eye remains in each piece.

Planting. The conventional planting method is to set seed pieces, cut side down, 4 inches deep, 12 inches apart in rows 24 to 36 inches apart. The tubers (what you eat) form on many stems rising from the seed piece. The potatoes do not grow in the roots. They form above the seed piece on underground stems. When plants are 5 to 6 inches high, scrape soil from between the rows and "hill-up" the plant (cover stems with soil). Potatoes exposed to light, either in the garden or storage, turn green and may become poisonous.

Growing. Apply fertilizer in bands at both sides of seed pieces at the time of planting. The best method is to make a 3-inch-deep, 6-inch-wide trench. Place seed pieces in a row in the center and work in fertilizer 1 to 2 inches deep at the edges of the trench.

Top: Loose soil makes it easy to harvest potatoes.

Potatoes can be grown in any container that's deep enough. Left: A plastic garbage can yields a good harvest.

Below: Plastic garbage bags are unlikely but successful containers for potato plants.

A steady supply of moisture is necessary. If the soil dries out after tubers begin to form, growth stops and a second growth starts when the soil becomes moist again. The result is knobby potatoes or multiples.

Alternate wet and dry conditions will also cause "hollow heart" (cavities near the center of the tuber).

Good tuber formation also requires cool nights. The complaint of "all tops and few potatoes" comes from gardeners who ignore the best planting dates in warm-summer areas.

Picking rather than digging. An old-time method of growing potatoes where you pick rather than dig is this: Set seed potatoes in a wide trench 3 inches deep. As stems grow, build up a covering of straw or pine needles or any material that will protect them from the sun. Cover the material with ½ inch of soil if wind is a problem. The potatoes will form almost at ground level and can be picked up by pulling back the straw. Early potatoes can be picked when tops begin to flower. They will reach full size when the tops die down.

Potato cultivars

Early-to-medium cultivars (90 to 110 days). 'Norland'. Very early. Red. Oblong, medium-sized tuber with shallow eyes. Used for baking, boiling. Some resistance to scab.

'Norgold Russet'. White. Oblong to long with shallow eyes and netted skin. Baking, boiling. Does not store well. Excellent resistance to scab.

'La Soda'. Red. Round. Boiling and potato salad. Does not store well. Good yields.

'White Rose'. White, long. Boiling, potato salad. Does not store well.

Late cultivars (110 to 140 days). 'Russet Burbank'. Very late. Long russet. Baking, frying, hash browns. Stores well. Doesn't grow well in hot areas.

'Kennebec'. White. Block-shaped. Good for frying and hash browns. Stores moderately well. Resistance to late blight, some scab.

'Red Pontiac'. Tends to become over-size with abundant rainfall. Fair table quality. Stores well.

Tree Tomatoes

Two types of tree tomatoes are available to the home gardener. They are quite different from the usual garden tomato that we all know. The domestic tree tomato—listed in seed company catalogs as 'Climbing Tomato', 'Trip-L-Crop', as well as 'Tree Tomato'—grows as a vigorous, indeterminate vine, capable of spreading to 18 feet. It produces large (a pound or more) smooth-skinned fruit. It is heavy-stemmed with potato-type leaves.

The subtropical tree tomato (*Cyphomandra betacea*), commonly called 'Tamarillo', has been promoted as an outdoor-indoor tree producing hundreds of tomatoes over a five-month period. In all but a subtropical climate it should be treated as an indoor plant. One such plant was donated to a local kindergarten classroom. It has never borne fruit (even though it is more than three years old). But it is prized for its exotic, elephant-ear-like leaves and waxy white blossoms. Taken from the classroom in summer, it receives a severe pruning back to a few sticks. When school resumes in the fall, the new foliage growth is full and fresh.

The fruit from commercial orchards in New Zealand is now being exported to California. The fruit is about the size of a large AA egg, tough-skinned, and quite tart.

Seed Sources

Listed below are several members of the nightshade family, relatives of the tomato. The numbers following each plant name refer to the numbered list of seed companies on pages 139–140, from which the plants may be ordered.

Peppers. Widely available. For unusual and hot pepper varieties, tomatillo, and so on, check (52).

Eggplant. Many varieties widely distributed. For Oriental varieties check (44), (45), (48), (56), (57).

Husk tomato. (4) (9) (12) (16) (20).

Potato. Check your garden store for local supply of certified seed potatoes. Availability: (9) (12) (16) (20) (50).

Tree tomato. Vine (4) (15) (16) (20) (21) (22) (31).

Tree tomato. Subtropical (31).

Don't make the mistake of planting too few eggplants—this versatile vegetable can be used in a variety of ways, including a hearty eggplant soup, the ingredients of which are shown here.

COOKING WITH TOMATOES

What is pleasing to the eye goes far in pleasing the palate. Happily, the proud achievement of harvest does not stop there: kitchen and table await in fitting climax.

For some gardeners the pleasure of growing the perfect tomato reaches its peak with frequent midsummer trips to the garden, salt shaker in hand, and the picking of a perfect, vine-ripe tomato. This juicy, sun-warmed bit of perfection marks the ultimate achievement and satisfaction for these tomato lovers.

For other gardeners, the pleasure of growing the perfect tomato is only a beginning. They know that many delicious uses are in store for that tomato, once a good cook takes over.

Take note of the advice and suggestions that follow and you will be well on your way to adding delicious tomatoes to your menus with ease and confidence.

☐ To ensure the best color, flavor, texture, and food value, cook tomatoes only until they are tender. Use a small amount of water; they create their own liquid as they cook. Also, the less water used, the more nutrients will be retained in the finished product.

☐ Use 1 pound of tomatoes for 4 half-cup servings of stewed tomatoes. The cooking time for this amount of cut-up tomatoes will be about 10 minutes.

☐ If you want to be slim and trim, add tomatoes to your diet. A 3½-ounce serving of raw tomatoes contains only 22 calories; a 1-cup serving of canned tomato juice contains 45 calories.

☐ When measuring tomatoes, either fresh or canned, the following equivalents will serve as a handy guide.

One pound of tomatoes consists of two large, three medium (2 by 2½ inches), or four small tomatoes.

One 8-ounce can equals 1 cup cooked tomatoes.

One 12-ounce can equals 1½ cups cooked tomatoes.

One 16-ounce can equals 2 cups cooked tomatoes.

One 28-ounce can equals 3½ cups cooked tomatoes.

One 46-ounce can of juice equals 5¾ cups.

One bushel of tomatoes (50 pounds) will make 20 quarts of cooked tomatoes.

☐ For the best flavor, ripe tomatoes should not be stored in the refrigerator for any length of time. As stated above, temperatures below 55°F. are damaging to the fruit. (Average refrigerator temperature is 45°F.) You will get top flavor if tomatoes are stored in a cool place at as close to 60°F. as possible.

☐ Make a practice of peeling and cutting tomatoes just before using them. If you must store peeled tomatoes, wrap them in wax paper, plastic wrap, or foil, and refrigerate.

To peel a tomato: (1) Cover with boiling water for 10 seconds. (2) Immerse in ice water until tomato has cooled. (3) Remove the peel using a serrated knife.

☐ Use the following guide when storing tomatoes.

Fresh, ripe, raw: cool place 60°F. or refrigerator no more than 2 to 3 days.

Fresh, cooked; canned, opened: refrigerator shelf 4 to 5 days.

Canned: kitchen shelf 1 year.

In cooked dishes, stored in refrigerator frozen-foods compartment, prepared for freezing: 2 to 3 months.

In cooked dishes stored in freezer at zero degrees: 1 year.

During the course of experimental tomato trials, Annette Fabri, an excellent chef with an inherited love for tomatoes, lent her talents. This chapter, in which Chef Fabri offers her suggestions and experience, includes recipes for and methods of preserving tomatoes.

"My first association with tomatoes was at a tender age. I remember, as a child, the jar of tomato sauce in my grandmother's icebox. I remember it well, because the sauce was used so often. Hers was the theory that almost any dish could be improved with a little tomato flavor or color. Her belief was passed on to my mother, and it is mine today.

"Although I have favorite herbs and spices that I use for seasoning, I am never without a jar of tomato sauce. When tomatoes are in season, I prepare a fresh tomato sauce, lightly seasoned with onion, bell pepper, and herbs. This will keep for about a week in my refrigerator. During the winter I substitute pints of home-canned tomato sauce for the fresh.

"I am fortunate in having a husband and son who share my fondness for tomatoes. We use them in everything from scrambled eggs to basting sauces for broiled and roasted meats to biscuit and bread dough.

"The versatility of the tomato has never ceased to amaze me. I have discovered that it is possible to take the tomato, in one form or another, through the entire sequence of a meal—from appetizer to dessert.

"Among the recipes that follow are some oldtime favorites, as well as some new recipes that use the tomato in less than traditional ways, from the first green tomatoes to the last of the abundant harvest."

Companion Herbs

The following herbs are the ones I reach for most often when there are tomatoes in the kitchen. Six herbs are just a starting point. You'll find the value of others by experimenting, as I did. That's half the fun of cooking.

Basil (*Ocimum basilicum*). The flavor of common sweet basil is like spicy cloves. It is one of the most delicate herbs and may be used more generously than the lustier ones. Whether fresh or dried, basil is the perfect complement to any tomato dish; the two flavors seem to have been made for each other.

Basil is of two basic kinds—sweet and bush. Sweet basil is an annual, growing 1 to 2 feet tall, with large 2-inch, glossy, dark green leaves. This basil is most commonly grown for cooking purposes.

Bush basil (*O. basilicum* 'Minimum') is a compact form that grows 6 to 12 inches tall, with tiny whitish flowers. The leaves are smaller than those of sweet basil, and the flavor milder. The most famous use for basil is pesto sauce.

Pesto sauce

One of the great sauces of Italy, this easily prepared combination of fresh basil, garlic, olive oil, and Parmesan cheese can be prepared in the blender and frozen in small individual amounts, to be used in a wide variety of ways.

2 cups firmly packed fresh basil leaves, rinsed well	½ cup olive oil
3 cloves garlic, peeled	1 cup shredded Parmesan cheese

Put basil in a blender jar; add garlic and olive oil and blend at a high speed until a very coarse purée is formed. Add cheese, a small amount at a time, until thoroughly blended. Makes about 1½ cups. Will keep for 1 week in a covered container in the refrigerator. For longer storage, drop into small mounds on foil, freeze, then package in a plastic bag, tightly wrapped.

To use, blend small amounts with butter, mayonnaise, or Italian-type salad dressing for use on fresh or cooked vegetables. Mix with cooked noodles, soups, stews, or cold seafood salads.

Coriander (*Coriandrum sativum*). The seeds of this small plant in the parsley family have a flavor resembling a combination of lemon peel and sage. The fresh or dried leaves are often sold as Chinese parsley or cilantro. The fresh leaves are a tasty and fragrant addition to mixed green salads and sliced fresh tomatoes.

Marjoram (*Origanum majorana*). This tender perennial is a member of the mint family. It has a fragrant aroma and a spicy taste similar to that of sage, though considerably less strong.

Dried marjoram is excellent used in a marinade for fresh sliced tomatoes.

Fresh basil leaves and sweet red onions complement slices of fresh tomato perfectly.

Spaghetti *al dente* with fresh pesto sauce.

Marinated tomato slices

6 medium tomatoes, peeled and sliced
¾ cup salad oil
¼ cup wine vinegar
2 tablespoons chopped green onion

1 teaspoon salt
Dash ground black pepper
2 teaspoons crushed dried marjoram

Place tomato slices in a deep bowl. Combine remaining ingredients, shaking well to blend thoroughly. Pour over tomatoes, cover, and chill for several hours, turning occasionally. Serves six.

Oregano (*Origanum vulgare*). This plant is among the more potent herbs and can be used in all tomato dishes. Fresh or dried leaves and tops are used. They have a sweet, aromatic flavor like that of sweet marjoram or thyme, though oregano is stronger and should be used with care. It is a favorite with Mexican and Italian cooks, and is often referred to as the "pizza herb."

Parsley (*Petroselinum crispum*). In this country, parsley, our most common herb, is of three main types—curled, plain-leaved, and turnip-rooted. Very popular is the moss curled variety, which has very dark green leaves, deeply curled, and is splendid for seasoning and general culinary decoration. Parsley leaves have a familiar, refreshing taste and aroma.

Bouquet garni

Parsley is an essential ingredient in a bouquet garni—a number of herbs and spices tied together in a cheesecloth bag so that they may be easily discarded after cooking. A bouquet garni is generally used in slow-cooking dishes such as soups and stews.

A basic bouquet garni is made with a few parsley sprigs, celery leaves, onion slices, and a sprig of thyme. However, depending on the dish to be flavored, any one or combination of other herbs and spices may be added—basil, garlic, chives, rosemary, tarragon, or whole cloves.

Thyme (*Thymus vulgaris*). A member of the mint family, this herb is moderately potent. It has a pungent flavor and sweet fragrance. It is one of the traditional herbs of Creole cuisine. Also, it is an essential ingredient in a bouquet garni.

Bottom: Ripe summer tomatoes in a fresh basil dressing.

Below: Bouquet garni is easily made for flavorful accents to soups and stews.

Whether fresh or canned, tomato sauce can be used as is, or as a base for many Italian sauces.

Sauces and Condiments

Many recipes in the following pages call for prepared products such as tomato sauce, stewed tomatoes, tomato juice, catsup, and tomato paste. These products are, of course, available at grocery stores and supermarkets, but by preparing them in my kitchen, I have the freedom to add my own touches. The following are some of my basic recipes for these products.

Tomato sauce

This sauce is the one I always have on hand in a jar in my refrigerator because it has a multitude of uses: on steaks, chops, and chicken before broiling; on leg of lamb and beef or pork roasts while roasting, to give a rich brown color. I also pour it over stuffed bell peppers, meat loaf, and baked fish. Combine it with scrambled eggs, fresh or frozen vegetables, baked rice, and include it in an endless number of casseroles. I use it when making biscuit and bread dough in place of some of the liquid normally called for, and as a base for Creole dishes, spaghetti sauce, barbecue sauces, soups, and salad dressings.

1 onion, chopped	3 cups peeled and chopped
2 tablespoons olive or salad oil	fresh tomatoes (or 3 cups
1 small clove garlic, crushed	canned, whole tomatoes)
2 tablespoons chopped parsley	1 teaspoon salt
¼ cup chopped green bell	½ teaspoon pepper
pepper	½ teaspoon dried oregano
	1 bay leaf

1. Cook onion in oil until lightly browned. Add garlic, parsley, and bell pepper and stir until vegetables are limp.
2. Add tomatoes, salt, pepper, oregano, and bay leaf. Simmer, uncovered, until thickened, about 1 hour.
3. Remove bay leaf and store sauce in covered container in refrigerator. Makes 2 cups.

Stewed tomatoes

6 medium-size ripe tomatoes	1 teaspoon white sugar
½ cup minced onion	1 tablespoon chopped parsley
¼ cup chopped green pepper	1 tablespoon butter
¼ cup chopped celery	Buttered bread crumbs
2 teaspoons salt	(optional)
½ teaspoon pepper	

1. Peel, core, and quarter tomatoes. Place in a saucepan together with onion, green pepper, and celery. Sprinkle with salt, pepper, sugar, and parsley.
2. Bring to a boil, cover, and simmer 10 minutes.
3. For serving as an individual dish, dot with butter and sprinkle with buttered crumbs. Makes four servings. Or use in combination with other ingredients in casseroles and stews.

Tomato paste

The best tomato paste is made with the Italian, plum-type tomatoes. It has many uses, and a small amount will go a long way. I use it to add color to otherwise pallid dishes, and for thickening tomato sauces.

1. Peel and chop 4 pounds of tomatoes. Measure and add 1 teaspoon salt for every pint of chopped tomatoes.
2. Place in a large kettle and simmer over low heat for about 1 hour. Stir often to keep from sticking.
3. Remove from heat and put through a food mill or fine sieve.
4. Return to kettle and continue to cook very slowly, until paste holds its shape on a spoon; takes about 2 hours. Stir occasionally to prevent sticking.
5. Pour into sterilized ½-pint jars, filling to within ½ inch from top. Seal and process in boiling-water bath for 30 minutes. (See pages 104–105.)

Homemade tomato paste is a main ingredient of Italian spaghetti sauce, and tastes better than the commercial version.

Cocktail sauce

This sauce is excellent for dunking small sausages or other hors d'oeuvres, or for garnishing shellfish.

¾ cup chili sauce or catsup (see below)
3 tablespoons lemon juice
3 tablespoons prepared horseradish
2 teaspoons Worcestershire sauce
1 teaspoon grated onion
Dash hot pepper sauce
Salt and pepper

1. Combine all ingredients. Add salt and pepper to taste. Chill.
2. Serve with seafood cocktails or as a dunking sauce. Makes 1½ cups.

Tomato catsup

You'll find many recipes for tomato catsup. The difference among most lies in the amount of spices used. The following is a typical recipe; the spices may be adjusted to suit one's own taste.

6 quarts (9 pounds) fresh, ripe tomatoes
3 medium onions, peeled and sliced
1 stalk celery, strings removed
2 large, sweet red peppers, seeded and sliced
2 cloves garlic, crushed
1 cup cider vinegar
1 teaspoon dry mustard
1 cup sugar
1 teaspoon paprika
1 tablespoon salt
1 teaspoon whole peppercorns
1 teaspoon whole cloves
2 teaspoons whole allspice
1 stick (2½ inches) cinnamon, broken

1. Remove stem and core from tomatoes; quarter. Place in a large kettle, together with onions, celery, and red peppers. Cook, uncovered, until soft, about 30 minutes.
2. Put through a food mill. Return pulp to kettle and add garlic, vinegar, mustard, sugar, paprika, and salt.
3. Tie whole spices in a cheesecloth bag and add to kettle.
4. Bring to a boil, lower heat, and simmer, uncovered, 1 hour or more, or until mixture is quite thick.
5. Remove spice bag. Pour into sterilized jars. Seal. Process in boiling-water bath 5 minutes. (See pages 104 and 105.) Makes about 2 pints.

Chili sauce

8 pounds ripe, juicy tomatoes
3 sweet red peppers
3 green bell peppers
1 stalk celery
2 cups chopped onion
2 cloves garlic, crushed
1 teaspoon *each:* whole allspice, mustard seed, whole cloves
1 cup light brown sugar
2 tablespoons salt
1 teaspoon *each:* fresh ground black pepper, dry mustard
2 dried, hot red peppers, crushed
1½ cups cider vinegar

1. Scald, peel, core, and chop the tomatoes. Chop peppers and celery. Add, with the onion and garlic, to the tomatoes. Bring to a boil and simmer for 45 minutes.
2. Tie whole spices in a cheesecloth bag and add to tomato mixture. Add brown sugar, salt, black pepper, mustard, and hot peppers. Boil, uncovered, until thick.
3. Add vinegar and boil the sauce until it has thickened to the correct consistency. Discard spice bag.
4. Pour into sterilized jars. Seal. Process in boiling-water bath for 5 minutes. (See pages 104 and 105.) Makes 8 pints.

Bright cherry tomatoes can be used as a garnish with beef ribs barbequed with a fresh tomato sauce.

All-purpose barbecue sauce

You'll want to keep this excellent barbecue sauce on hand. The recipe makes a large amount, but sauce keeps for months in the refrigerator. We use it for all meats; it is especially good on poultry.

½ cup chopped onion	½ cup prepared mustard
¼ cup olive oil	¼ cup sugar
2 cups sauterne wine	Salt and pepper to taste
1 cup soy sauce	¼ cup chopped parsley
2 cups catsup	

1. Cook onion in olive oil for 5 minutes.
2. Add wine and simmer until reduced by half.
3. Add remaining ingredients, except parsley, and simmer for 20 minutes. Do not boil at any time.
4. Remove from heat and add parsley. Adjust seasoning to taste.
5. Pour into a jar and keep refrigerated until needed. Makes 1 quart.
6. To use, brush on meat about 15 minutes before barbecuing. Use as a basting sauce while meat is cooking.

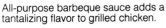
All-purpose barbeque sauce adds a tantalizing flavor to grilled chicken.

Fresh tomato barbecue sauce

This basic barbecue sauce can be used on all meats. Variations are possible, depending on taste preferences.

½ cup chopped onion	⅛ teaspoon hot pepper sauce
1 clove garlic, crushed	1 teaspoon dry mustard
½ cup salad oil	2 tablespoons brown sugar
2 cups peeled, seeded, and chopped tomatoes	1 teaspoon dried oregano
	½ cup dry red wine
2 tablespoons lemon juice	Salt and pepper to taste

1. Sauté onion and garlic in oil. Add tomatoes and simmer until soft.
2. Add remaining ingredients, except wine, and simmer gently for 30 minutes, or until thickened.
3. Add the wine and heat thoroughly. Season with salt and pepper.
4. Cool slightly. Poor into blender and whirl until smooth. Store in refrigerator in covered container. Makes 3 cups.

Variations

☐ Substitute dried thyme or basil for the oregano.
☐ Stir in a bit of chili sauce just before the sauce is ready to serve.
☐ Substitute an equal amount of white sugar for brown.
☐ Sauté half a green pepper, chopped, with the onion and garlic.

Tomato juice

Select tomatos that are ripe and juicy. Wash; remove stems and cores. Cut into quarters. Simmer in a large kettle until soft, stirring often. Put through a food mill or fine sieve to remove peel and seeds. Season to taste.

Refrigerate small amounts in covered container for up to 1 week.

Larger amounts should be processed for canning, as follows: Add one teaspoon salt to each quart of juice. Reheat to boiling and pour immediately into sterilized jars, filling to within ½ inch of top. Seal, screw bands firmly tight. Process in boiling-water bath for 10 minutes. (See pages 104–105.)

Tomato-vegetable cocktail

2 cups tomato juice, canned or fresh	Few parsley sprigs
1 carrot, cut up	1 cup crushed ice
¼ small onion	Dash Worcestershire sauce
Few celery leaves	¼ teaspoon bottled horseradish

1. Combine all ingredients in a blender.
2. Cover and whirl until blended and smooth.
3. Serve immediately. Serves four.

Fresh tomato juice is easily prepared, low in calories, and deliciously thirst-quenching.

Tomato juice cocktail

3 cups tomato juice, fresh or
canned
⅛ teaspoon pepper
¾ teaspoon salt

¼ teaspoon sugar
1 tablespoon lemon juice
4 drops hot pepper sauce

1. Combine all ingredients in a large pitcher. Chill thoroughly.
2. Stir well and serve in chilled glasses—with lemon wedges, if desired.
   Serves six.

Spicy tomato juice cocktail

1 cucumber, peeled and grated
6 cups tomato juice, fresh or
canned
3 green onions, finely chopped
3 tablespoons lemon juice
Dash hot pepper sauce

1 tablespoon Worcestershire sauce
1 tablespoon bottled
horseradish
Salt and pepper to taste

1. Combine all ingredients in a large pitcher and chill at least 2 hours.
2. Strain through a coarse sieve.
3. Stir well and pour into chilled glasses. Serves eight.

Tomato pick-up

We encountered this fresh, spicy drink in Mexico.

3 cups tomato juice
1 cup orange juice
1 fresh or canned green chili,
seeds and vein removed

1 teaspoon sugar
½ teaspoon salt
Juice of 1 small lime
¼ cup chopped white onion

1. Place all ingredients in a blender and whirl until combined.
2. Chill thoroughly.
3. Serve in chilled wine glasses.

Soups and Salads

A refreshing way to begin a meal is with a bowl of homemade tomato soup
or a fresh tomato salad.

Fresh tomato aspic

3 tablespoons plain gelatin
½ cup cold water
8 large tomatoes
1 teaspoon sugar
1 bay leaf
1 teaspoon salt

2 small onions, coarsely
chopped
1 stalk celery, coarsely
chopped
1 teaspoon peppercorns
3 tablespoons lemon juice
⅛ teaspoon hot pepper sauce

1. Sprinkle gelatin in water to soften.
2. Quarter tomatoes, cutting away white core and stem end. You should
   have about 2 quarts.
3. Place tomatoes in a saucepan and add sugar, bay leaf, salt, onions, celery,
   and peppercorns. Cook over low heat until tomatoes are soft, about
   10 minutes.
4. Strain through a food mill and measure 5 cups of tomato juice. If amount
   is less than 5 cups, add enough water, canned tomato juice, consommé, or
   bouillon to make 5 cups.
5. Add softened gelatin to hot tomato juice and stir to dissolve; then add
   lemon juice, hot pepper sauce, and salt and pepper to taste.
6. Turn into lightly greased 5- to 6-cup mold. Chill until firm.

Variations. Adding other fruits, vegetables, meat, poultry, or fish to this
recipe provides an almost infinite variety of zesty tastes and textures.

Tomato-vegetable aspic

Follow steps 1 through 5; then chill mixture until consistency of unbeaten egg white. Fold in 1 cup shredded cabbage, ½ cup chopped celery, and 1 cup finely chopped green pepper. Turn into 7- to 8-cup mold. Chill until firm.

Other variations. Follow directions for tomato-vegetable aspic, but substitute one of the following for the raw vegetables:

☐ 1½ cups cooked vegetables
☐ 1 cup diced cooked chicken and ¼ cup sliced olives
☐ 1 cup cooked shrimp
☐ 1 cup slivered cooked ham and ¼ cup pickle relish

Cream of fresh tomato soup

2½ cups chopped ripe tomatoes	2 tablespoons butter or
1 medium onion, sliced	margarine
1 bay leaf	2 tablespoons all-purpose
1 teaspoon salt	flour
¼ teaspoon pepper	2 cups milk
	Chopped fresh basil

1. Simmer tomatos with onion, bay leaf, salt, and pepper, for 10 minutes, then strain.
2. Make a white sauce by melting butter and blending with the flour. Gradually add the milk and cook over low heat until slightly thick, stirring constantly.
3. Just before serving, slowly add hot, strained tomatoes to the white sauce, stirring until smooth. Garnish with fresh basil. Serves four.

Chilled Spanish gazpacho uses tomato juice in two ways—as a liquid ingredient, and frozen in cubes to keep the soup cold.

Hot tomato bouillon

This first-course soup is always welcome on a cold winter day. I like to serve it in large mugs, with a sprinkling of crumbled bacon on top. The horseradish is a nice tangy addition.

1½ cups tomato juice, fresh or canned
1 can condensed beef broth
1 cup water
¼ cup egg pastina (tiny soup macaroni)

½ teaspoon prepared horseradish
2 slices bacon, crisp-cooked, drained, and crumbled.

1. In a saucepan, combine tomato juice, beef broth, water, pastina, and horseradish. Bring to a boil and simmer 7 to 10 minutes or until pastina is tender, stirring occasionally.
2. Ladle into large mugs and spoon crumbled bacon on top. Serves four.

Gazpacho

Many versions of this cold Spanish tomato soup recommend that all the ingredients be put through a blender rather than be chopped by hand. I prefer to combine both methods, allowing the flavor of each vegetable to be more distinct and giving the soup a nice texture. A good way to keep this soup icy cold is to freeze cubes of plain tomato juice and add them to the gazpacho just before serving.

1 medium cucumber, peeled, seeded, and chopped
1 large green pepper, seeded and chopped
2 stalks celery, pared to remove any strings, and bias cut
½ cup green onion, chopped
1 clove garlic
2 tablespoons chopped parsley
½ teaspoon dried basil (or 2 tablespoons fresh)

2 cups tomato juice, fresh or canned
4 tablespoons olive oil
3 tablespoons vinegar or lemon juice
4 large ripe tomatoes, peeled, seeded, and chopped
Dash of hot pepper sauce
Salt and pepper to taste

Condiments: Croutons, minced green onions, chopped bell pepper, chopped hard-boiled egg, sour cream, frozen cubes of tomato juice

1. Place all ingredients except tomatoes, hot pepper sauce, salt, pepper, and condiments into blender. Whirl only until blended, but not pulverized.
2. Pour into large container and add tomatoes, hot pepper sauce, salt, and pepper. Taste and adjust seasoning if necessary.
3. Chill thoroughly.
4. Place condiments in individual bowls, to be passed separately. Serves six.

Fresh tomato soup

I am particularly fond of tomato soups, both hot and chilled. We have several favorites, and I have always been able to make one to complement the main course of just about any meal I serve.

I've found that fresh, fully ripe, tomatoes make the best tomato soups. However, when fresh tomatoes are out of season, canned tomatoes, peeled, can be substituted.

½ cup butter
2 tablespoons salad oil
1 large onion, thinly sliced
3 pounds ripe tomatoes, peeled, cored, and quartered
2 teaspoons chopped fresh thyme (or ½ teaspoon dried)
2 tablespoons chopped fresh basil (or 1 teaspoon dried)

3 tablespoons canned tomato paste
¼ cup all-purpose flour
4 cups rich chicken broth
1 cup cream
1 teaspoon sugar
Salt and pepper to taste

1. Heat butter and oil in a heavy skillet. Add the onion and cook until translucent.
2. In a large kettle combine tomatos, herbs, onion (and oil and butter), and tomato paste. Simmer for 10 minutes.
3. Mix the flour with ¾ cup of the chicken broth and stir into the tomato mixture. Add remaining broth and cook 30 minutes, stirring frequently.
4. Pass mixture through a fine sieve or whirl in blender until smooth. Reheat and stir in cream and sugar. Do not boil. Add salt and pepper to taste.
5. Serve in cups or bowls with a pat of butter, if desired. Serves eight.

Left: Tomato-vegetable beef soup, plus bread and a salad, makes an elegant, hearty, and inexpensive meal.

Opposite: Thick and hearty, sherried tomato seafood bisque is an easily prepared main course.

Tomato-vegetable beef soup

This very thick, hearty soup uses a variety of fresh vegetables. Lima beans, chopped cabbage, diced yellow turnip, cauliflower, or whatever you happen to have on hand can be substituted for the vegetables listed.

1 beef soup bone
1 pound soup beef, cubed
1 tablespoon salt
½ teaspoon peppercorns
1 bay leaf
2 quarts water
1 medium onion, chopped
2 large carrots, diced
3 celery stalks, sliced

1 cup *each* of cut green beans, corn, green peas, and diced potatoes
2½ cups peeled and quartered tomatoes
1 medium green pepper, diced
Salt and pepper to taste

1. Put soup bone, meat, salt, peppercorns, bay leaf, and 2 quarts of water in a large kettle. Bring to boil; simmer, covered, for 1 hour.
2. Add vegetables; bring to boil and simmer, covered, for 1 hour longer.
3. Remove meat from bone and put meat back in soup.
4. Season with salt and pepper to taste. Makes about 2½ quarts.

Sherried tomato seafood bisque

I like to use various wines in my cooking and find sherry to be one of the most versatile—it is especially good in this seafood bisque, if added just before serving. I also serve a cruet of sherry along with the soup, should any of my guests wish to add more. This hearty soup can be made with either crab, shrimp, or lobster. Served with hot garlic-buttered French bread and a tossed green salad, it becomes a meal in itself.

4½ cups peeled tomatoes
2 cups beef broth (or use beef bouillon cubes and water, or canned beef bouillon)
1 cup diced celery
2 small onions, sliced
2 small carrots, sliced
3 tablespoons uncooked rice
2 parsley sprigs
4 whole cloves
6 peppercorns

Small piece of bay leaf
Pinch of ground thyme
2 teaspoons salt
1½ pounds crab meat, shrimp, or lobster, cooked and cut into pieces
2 cups light cream
Sherry to taste
Thin slices of lemon and chopped parsley for garnish
Croutons

1. Put tomatoes, broth, vegetables, rice, and seasonings (tie seasonings in a cheese cloth bag) into a kettle. Bring to a boil, cover, and simmer for 1 hour.
2. Remove from heat and discard cheesecloth bag. Put all ingredients into a blender and whirl until smooth.
3. Just before serving add fish; simmer until heated through.
4. Heat cream slightly and add to tomato mixture. Season to taste.
5. Add a dash of sherry; garnish with lemon slices and chopped parsley. Serve at once. Pass croutons and extra sherry. Serves eight.

A bowl of ice cubes keeps creamy iced tomato soup chilled and ready to serve.

Creamy iced tomato soup

This soup, one of the best cold soups I know of, is surprisingly easy to prepare. It can be made as much as 2 days in advance. Stir in sour cream just before serving.

2 large ripe tomatoes, peeled and quartered	½ teaspoon pepper
1 small clove garlic, crushed	2 cups tomato juice, fresh or canned
1 teaspoon sugar	1 cup dairy sour cream
1 tablespoon salt	1 large cucumber

1. Press quartered tomatoes through a sieve into a large bowl.
2. Add garlic, sugar, salt, pepper, and the 2 cups of tomato juice. Cover and refrigerate. (Stop here if you are working ahead.)
3. When ready to serve, taste and add additional seasonings, if necessary. If mixture is too thick, stir in additional tomato juice. Stir in sour cream until blended and smooth.
4. Serve chilled soup in cups or bowls, garnished with cucumber slices. Serves six.

Chilled beef and tomato salad

Leftover boiled beef or pot roast are ideal for this chilled salad. Prepare it a day ahead, so all ingredients can marinate thoroughly.

3 medium boiled potatoes, peeled	½ cup Italian dressing
2 large tomatoes, peeled, seeded, and cut into chunks	1 teaspoon Worcestershire sauce
3 cups boiled beef, cut into strips	2 teaspoons chopped onion
1 tablespoon minced parsley	1 teaspoon oregano
	Salt and pepper to taste

1. Cut potatoes and tomatoes into medium-size chunks.
2. Mix all ingredients in a large bowl. Season to taste, cover, and chill overnight.
3. Serve on a cold platter, lined with lettuce leaves. Serves four.

Mexican tomato salad

This salad can be prepared well ahead of serving time. If fresh coriander is unavailable, the same amount of parsley can be substituted. However, the coriander adds greatly to the distinct south-of-the-border flavor.

2 pounds medium-size zucchini

4 hard-boiled eggs

4 large, fresh, firm ripe tomatoes, peeled, seeded, and diced

½ cup olive or salad oil

1 teaspoon finely minced green chilies

¼ cup finely minced green onions

1 tablespoon minced coriander

3 tablespoons wine vinegar

Salt and pepper to taste

1. Cut zucchini in half lengthwise, then into ¼-inch pieces. Do not peel. Boil in salted water for 5 minutes. Drain well.
2. Cut eggs into large pieces. Place zucchini, eggs, and tomatoes in salad bowl. Add oil and combine thoroughly.
3. Add chili peppers, green onions, coriander, vinegar, and seasonings. Toss well, cover, and chill till serving time. Serves six.

Antipasto salad

Antipasto salad is fun to make. I start with a border of lettuce, either head lettuce or romaine, and sliced tomatoes. In the center of the platter, I give free rein to my imagination in trying to arrange colorful combinations of food—thinly sliced meats and cheeses for a delightful contrast, salami, hard-cooked eggs, tuna, olives (both green and black), artichoke hearts, anchovy fillets, and even pickled beets and sweet red peppers can be added for color. I like to make up combinations that include favorite delicacies of each of my guests. For a large party I make two or three different antipasto trays. The combinations are endless.

In addition to the above, consider some of the following when preparing an antipasto tray:

☐ Marinated mushrooms
☐ Pickled oysters
☐ Stuffed celery
☐ Sardines in olive oil

☐ Slices of fresh kohlrabi
☐ Small green onions
☐ Radish flowerettes
☐ Boiled shrimp or crabmeat

This antipasto salad makes liberal use of thick tomato slices sprinkled with herbs.

Above: Wedge-sliced tomatoes stuffed with peas and shrimp.

Opposite: A variety of stuffed tomato fillings, with a variety of slicings.

Cold stuffed tomato salads

Fresh tomato salads are a real hit for a summer luncheon. I like to cut each tomato in a different way and use a variety of stuffings. I then set the salads out on a buffet table where guests can choose their favorites. If I am serving them as a side dish instead of a main course, I cut the tomatoes in halves or slices, place a ring of bell pepper, ½ inch or more thick, on each slice, and fill the ring. The contrast of the filling with the bright green ring in the middle and the beautiful red tomato on the bottom is very pretty.

Whether or not to peel a tomato which is to be stuffed depends a great deal on its appearance. If it is good and ripe, it doesn't need peeling. However, if it appears to be coarse and the color is inconsistent, by all means peel. To prepare tomato cases, first peel the tomatoes, if you choose, then hollow them—a serrated grapefruit spoon greatly speeds the process. Sprinkle lightly with salt, invert, and allow to drain for 20 minutes. Chill, then fill with stuffing of your choice. A few suggestions follow:

☐ Tiny shrimp that have been marinated in Italian dressing. Drain and sprinkle with parsley.
☐ Cottage cheese seasoned with chopped, canned green chilies, pimento, onion, and a dash of Worcestershire.
☐ Guacamole mixed with chunks of fresh avocado.
☐ Hard-boiled eggs, mashed and seasoned with mayonnaise and curry powder.
☐ Potato or macaroni salad seasoned with onion, green pepper, and hard-boiled eggs.
☐ Tuna fish and a garlic-flavored mayonnaise dressing.
☐ Chicken salad mixed with crisp celery chunks and a mayonnaise dressing.
☐ Cold salmon garnished with cucumber slices and served with lemon wedges.
☐ Crab or lobster chunks marinated in a little vinaigrette sauce before filling. Serve additional sauce on the side.
☐ Crabmeat and a Louis dressing, served with sliced beets, hard-boiled eggs, and asparagus spears.

Above: Whole cherry tomatoes garnish this vegetable rice ring; chopped, they add flavor to the ring itself.

Opposite: Tomatoes combine well with other vegetables to make delicious, versatile relishes.

Vegetable rice ring

This salad is a real time-saver for me, even though it looks as if it might take a long time to prepare. I cook the rice a day ahead and marinate it overnight in Italian dressing. It's always fun to experiment with different raw vegetables to add to it. Bright little cherry tomatoes in the center of the mold not only look good but they also add an extra special flavor.

2 cups cooked rice
½ cup Italian salad dressing
½ cup mayonnaise or salad dressing
1 cup sliced radishes
1 medium cucumber, seeded and chopped

2 small tomatoes, peeled, seeded, and chopped
1 medium green pepper, chopped
½ cup chopped celery
¼ cup chopped green onions
Leaf lettuce
1 pint cherry tomatoes

1. Combine cooked rice and Italian salad dressing; cover and chill several hours or overnight.
2. Add mayonnaise to undrained rice mixture and stir until combined.
3. Fold in radishes, cucumber, tomatoes, green pepper, celery, and green onions.
4. Press into 5½-cup ring mold that has been greased lightly with salad oil.
5. Cover; refrigerate at least 2 to 3 hours.
6. To serve, unmold onto lettuce-lined platter and fill center with cherry tomatoes. Makes eight to ten servings.

Relishes and Side Dishes

You can choose among many types of tomato relishes. You can enjoy some fresh and can others. I like to make fresh relishes during the summer when so many fresh vegetables are available. They will keep for several days in the refrigerator. Both fresh and canned relishes are excellent served with hamburgers, hot dogs, and barbecued and broiled meats.

Fresh tomato salsa

For a "something different" relish or appetizer, serve this fresh tomato salsa with corn chips. The fresh vegetables mixed with chopped green chilies and spices get dinner or cocktails off to an extra spicy start.

4 medium tomatoes, peeled and finely chopped	2 to 3 tablespoons canned green chilis, drained and finely chopped
½ cup finely chopped onion	2 tablespoons red wine vinegar
½ cup finely chopped celery	1 teaspoon mustard seed
¼ cup finely chopped green pepper	1 teaspoon crushed coriander seed
¼ cup olive oil or salad oil	1 teaspoon salt
	Dash pepper

1. Combine all ingredients.
2. Cover. Chill several hours or overnight; stir occasionally.

Tomato, pepper, and celery relish

3 medium tomatoes	2 tablespoons *each* of vinegar and sugar
1 green pepper, minced	½ cup cold water
½ cup diced celery	⅛ teaspoon salt
1 small onion, minced	
1½ teaspoons salt	

1. Peel and dice tomatoes. Combine with remaining ingredients.
2. Chill for several hours. Drain. Makes 2 cups.

Tomato, onion, and cucumber relish

2 tomatoes, sliced in thin wedges	2 tablespoons chopped parsley
2 onions, chopped	½ cup Italian salad dressing
1 medium cucumber, peeled and sliced	Salt and pepper to taste

1. Place vegetables and parsley in a shallow bowl. Pour dressing over the top and mix lightly.
2. Allow to marinate and chill thoroughly.
3. Drain. Add salt and pepper to taste. Makes 2 cups.

Fresh tomato salsa adds zest to Mexican food or can be used as a spicy preprandial dip.

Wine-glazed tomatoes

Wine and a brown sugar-butter sauce make this an outstanding vegetable dish to serve with roast beef or steak. If you do not have fresh basil, substitute chopped parsley.

4 large tomatoes	1 teaspoon salt
4 tablespoons butter or margarine	½ cup white or rosé wine
2 tablespoons brown sugar	Pepper
	Chopped fresh basil

1. Slice tomatoes into ¼-inch rounds.
2. In large skillet, combine butter and brown sugar and stir until melted. Add salt.
3. Add tomato slices and cook quickly on both sides. Add wine and simmer 1 to 2 minutes or until tomatoes are heated through, basting with the wine sauce.
4. Sprinkle with pepper and chopped basil. Serve in small dishes. Serves six to eight.

Baked macaroni and tomatoes

Tomatoes, macaroni, and Cheddar cheese combine nicely in this dish. I serve it with broiled hamburgers and a fresh fruit salad. The tomatoes eliminate the need for another vegetable.

1 package (8 ounces) macaroni	2½ cups peeled, seeded, and chopped fresh tomatoes
2 tablespoons butter or margarine	1 teaspoon salt
3 tablespoons chopped onion	½ cup grated sharp Cheddar cheese
1 medium bell pepper, chopped	

1. Cook macaroni in boiling salted water until tender. Drain thoroughly.
2. Cook onion and bell pepper in butter until tender. Add tomatoes and simmer about 5 minutes.
3. Add drained macaroni and salt. Mix well and simmer 10 minutes longer.
4. Arrange half of macaroni-tomato mixture in bottom of a greased casserole. Sprinkle with half of the grated cheese. Add remaining macaroni-tomato mixture and sprinkle top with remaining grated cheese.
5. Bake in a 400°F. oven until cheese is nicely browned, about 15 minutes. Serves six.

Scalloped tomatoes

Buttered bread crumbs and hot pepper sauce add greatly to this tasty dish. During the winter, when fresh tomatoes are not available, I substitute canned whole tomatoes, but drain off a bit of the liquid.

1 tablespoon butter or margarine	1 teaspoon sugar
2 teaspoons minced onion	1 teaspoon salt
¼ cup dried green pepper	1 tablespoon flour
¼ teaspoon hot pepper sauce	½ cup buttered bread crumbs
3 cups peeled and quartered tomatoes	

1. Melt butter in saucepan. Add onion and green pepper; cook until tender, but not brown.
2. Stir in hot pepper sauce; add tomatoes, sugar, salt, and flour. Bring to a boil; reduce heat and simmer 10 minutes.
3. Turn into a greased 1-quart casserole. Sprinkle with buttered bread crumbs. Bake in 375°F. oven until crumbs are nicely browned, about 15 minutes. Serves four.

Vegetable medley

During the summer when our garden abounds with fresh vegetables, I like to make up combinations of vegetables and seasonings, such as this one. Use this basic recipe; add or delete other vegetables, depending on what is in season at the time—bell peppers, carrots, celery, or zucchini, for instance. It always tastes different and is a great dish to serve with simply prepared meats.

Opposite: Vegetable medley uses different ingredients according to the season, but tomatoes play a central role.

1 large onion, sliced
1 clove garlic, minced
¼ cup minced parsley
2 teaspoons salt
½ teaspoon *each* pepper, ground thyme, and dried basil (substitute 1 tablespoon fresh basil leaves, if available)

2 tablespoons cooking oil
1 pound green beans, cut
3 large tomatoes, quartered
2 cups diced summer squash, sliced 1 inch thick

1. Cook onion, garlic, parsley, and seasonings in oil in a large skillet for 3 minutes.
2. Add beans with ½ cup water and simmer, covered, for 10 minutes.
3. Add remaining vegetables, cover, and cook until tender but crisp. Don't overcook. Makes four to six servings.

Tomatoes Florentine

With this recipe, I turn spinach into a special event. We like these stuffed tomatoes with just about any kind of roasted meat. If you want to prepare them ahead of time, refrigerate the stuffed tomatoes until ready to cook, and add 10 minutes to the cooking time.

6 medium tomatoes
½ teaspoon salt
12 ounces fresh spinach or 2 packages (10 ounces each) frozen chopped spinach

2 tablespoons butter or margarine
2 tablespoons all-purpose flour
¾ cup milk
2 hard-boiled eggs

1. Cut a slice, ¼ inch thick, off the top of each tomato. Scoop out the insides of tomatoes, leaving a shell about ¼ inch thick. Sprinkle insides with salt and set aside.
2. Cook fresh spinach in small amount of boiling water 5 to 8 minutes. Drain well; chop and return to saucepan. (Or prepare frozen spinach according to package directions; drain well.) Add butter or margarine; stir until melted.
3. Blend together flour and milk; add to spinach. Cook and stir until thickened and bubbly.
4. Sieve one hard-cooked egg yolk and set aside. Chop remaining egg and egg white and add to creamed spinach.
5. Fill tomatoes with spinach mixture. Place in a shallow baking dish. Bake at 375°F. for 20 minutes.
6. Sprinkle tops of tomatoes with sieved egg yolk just before serving. Serves six.

Barbecued tomatoes

Although cherry tomatoes seem like the ideal size for skewering, their tough skin and weak flavor are always a disappointment.

With a sharp knife, remove stems from medium-size, firm, ripe tomatoes. Cut each tomato in half, crosswise. Stab tomatoes with two skewers, brush with oil, and lay skewers over glowing coals. Rotate occasionally, until warmed through. The double-skewer method will keep tomatoes from revolving when turned.

Main Dishes and Casseroles

For elegant entertaining or simple family fare, tomatoes will add new taste appeal to many favorite casseroles. Following are some of my favorites.

Tomato fish stew

My Italian grandmother always served a thick, robust fish stew (actually more like a soup) during the Lenten Season. I've changed her recipe a bit by using a wider variety of fish and lacing the stew with white wine just before serving. Hot toasted French bread, for dunking, and a tossed green salad complete the meal.

6 slices bacon, diced	⅛ teaspoon pepper
¾ cup chopped onion	½ teaspoon oregano
1 clove garlic, minced	¼ teaspoon basil
¾ cup bias cut celery	1 bay leaf
¼ cup diced green pepper	1 pound halibut fillets
2 cups peeled and chopped tomatoes	½ pound fillet of sole
1 cup tomato sauce	½ pound red snapper
1 cup water	¼ pound codfish
3 potatoes, peeled and cut into large chunks	¼ pound shrimp, raw and peeled
2 teaspoons salt	1 cup white wine
	Parsley for garnish

1. Fry bacon in large saucepan until it is limp.
2. Add vegetables, except potatoes, tomatoes, and tomato sauce, and cook until translucent.
3. Add tomatos, tomato sauce, water, potatoes, and seasonings.
4. Cover and cook about 20 minutes, or until potatoes are tender.
5. Cut fish into bite-size pieces and add to tomato mixture.
6. Cover and continue cooking 5 to 8 minutes, until fish is done. Remove bay leaf.
7. Add wine; sprinkle with chopped parsley garnish. Serves six.

Italian spaghetti sauce

I always have a container of spaghetti sauce on hand in my freezer. It is what I call my "convenience food." If I'm preparing the sauce for freezing, I omit the meat. This way I can use it in any number of ways—for Swiss steak, as a pizza sauce, for lasagna, in Eggplant Parmesan, or by adding clams, chicken, or seafood, as another type of spaghetti sauce.

3 tablespoons olive oil	1½ teaspoons oregano
1 clove garlic, minced	¼ teaspoon thyme
1 celery stalk, chopped	3 fresh basil leaves (or ½ teaspoon dried)
1 carrot, chopped	1 bay leaf
1 large onion, chopped	1 can (3 ounces) chopped mushrooms, including liquid
1 small bell pepper, chopped	
¼ cup chopped parsley	
½ pound ground beef	1 tablespoon salt
2 cups peeled, chopped tomatoes	½ teaspoon pepper
1 can (8 ounces) tomato sauce	1 teaspoon sugar
2 tablespoons tomato paste	½ cup Burgundy wine
1 cup water	

1. Sauté garlic, vegetables (except tomatoes), parsley, and meat in olive oil until vegetables are tender and meat is lightly browned.
2. Add tomatoes, tomato sauce, tomato paste, and water, and cook together gently for a few minutes.
3. Add herbs, mushrooms, and seasonings and simmer, uncovered, for 2 to 2½ hours, or until thickened. Add wine and adjust seasonings, if necessary; remove bay leaf. Makes approximately 2 quarts.

Tomato fish stew combines fish and a variety of vegetables in a rich tomato sauce.

Spareribs, tomatoes, and green beans casserole

This very old and delicious recipe has been in our family for many years. It is a one-pot meal that I prepare often during the summer, when both tomatoes and green beans are in season. Fresh tomatoes mingled with the meat juice transform the liquid into a good, rich gravy.

3 pounds lean, meaty spareribs (have butcher cut rack in half, lengthwise)	1 cup peeled and chopped tomatoes
1 onion, chopped	1 pound green beans
1 tablespoon chopped parsley	4 potatoes, peeled and quartered
1 teaspoon oregano	Salt and pepper to taste
2 cups warm water	

1. Cut spareribs into individual pieces and sauté in a small amount of oil or butter in a large pot or Dutch oven, together with onion, salt, pepper, parsley, and oregano.
2. When onions are translucent and spareribs are lightly browned, add water and tomatoes and cook for 20 minutes.
3. Add green beans, cover, and cook for another 20 minutes.
4. Add potatoes, cover, and cook an additional 20 minutes or until potatoes are tender. If necessary, remove cover towards end of cooking period and allow gravy to thicken. Salt and pepper to taste. Serves six.

To fry green tomato slices, dip them first in flour, then in egg, and then in seasoned bread crumbs (right), then fry them slowly until they are crisp and golden brown (far right).

Opposite: Creamy tomato rarebit is delicious over tomato halves and English muffins.

Fried green tomato slices

I've tried several ways of frying green tomatoes and this method, by far, is the best. The bread crumbs take on a rich, golden color and become crisp, while the tomatoes inside stay firm but tender.

6 medium-size green tomatoes, sliced ¼ inch thick
½ cup all-purpose flour
2 beaten eggs
1 cup seasoned bread crumbs (season with salt, pepper, parsley, chopped onion, and dried oregano)

1. Dip tomato slices first in flour, then in egg, then in seasoned bread crumbs.
2. Cook in a small amount of oil, in a large skillet, over medium heat, until lightly browned, about 3 minutes on each side. Tomatoes should be tender when pierced with a fork, but not overdone.
3. Drain on absorbent paper. Serve warm, with lemon wedges, if desired.

Tomato rarebit

A favorite combination of mine is cheese and tomatoes. In this dish I sometimes sprinkle buttered bread crumbs over the tomatoes just before broiling them. Also, adding 2 tablespoons of dry sherry to the rarebit just before serving gives it a nice nutty flavor.

3 tomatoes, cut in half crosswise
Salt, pepper, and sugar to taste
Bread crumbs (optional)
2 tablespoons butter
1 tablespoon prepared mustard
½ teaspoon dry mustard
½ teaspoon paprika
¼ teaspoon salt
¼ teaspoon curry powder
2 teaspoons Worcestershire sauce
1 pound Cheddar cheese, cut into ½-inch cubes
½ cup beer
2 egg yolks
¼ cup cream
2 tablespoons dry sherry (optional)
English muffins or toast triangles

1. Sprinkle tomatoes with salt, pepper, sugar, and breadcrumbs. Broil until tender and heated through, about 10 minutes. Keep warm while preparing sauce.
2. In the top part of a chafing dish or double boiler, place butter to melt. Add prepared mustard, dry mustard, paprika, salt, curry powder, and Worcestershire sauce. Stir well.
3. Add cheese, stirring constantly until melted. Keep water in the lower part of chafing dish or double boiler simmering, but not boiling. If it boils rapidly, it may cause the cheese to become stringy.
4. When cheese has melted, add beer and stir through. Continue cooking until mixture is very hot and thoroughly blended.
5. Beat egg yolks with cream and slowly add to the cheese, stirring constantly.
6. Remove from heat. Stir in sherry, if desired.
7. Place broiled tomatoes on top of muffins or toast and pour hot rarebit over. Serve immediately. Serves six.

Baked tomatoes stuffed with croutons, cheese, and herbs, are arranged around a roasted chicken for an elegant meal.

Baked tomatoes

4 medium to large ripe tomatoes
1 to 1½ cups unseasoned croutons
Juice of ½ lemon
½ teaspoon dried basil
1 tablespoon chopped parsley
1 teaspoon fresh chives
¼ teaspoon garlic salt
Salt and pepper to taste
4 tablespoons grated Parmesan cheese
2 tablespoons butter

1. Remove a slice from the top of each tomato and scoop out the inside to within ½ inch of the shell.
2. Chop tomato pulp into bite-size pieces and combine with remaining ingredients, except cheese and butter, blending only until croutons are moistened.
3. Refill tomato shells with mixture, packing lightly.
4. Sprinkle with grated cheese and dot with butter.
5. Place in lightly oiled baking dish and bake in 350°F. oven for 20 minutes.
6. Remove from oven and place under broiler for additional 5 minutes or until nicely browned on top. Serves four.

Another use for baked tomatoes—as an accompaniment for boned leg of lamb.

Breads

These breads are excellent toasted and add a nice flavor to sandwiches.

Tomato bread

This bread is a beautiful orange-red color.

1 package active dry yeast	2 tablespoons butter
¼ cup warm water (105–115°F.)	2 teaspoons salt
¼ teaspoon sugar	2 tablespoons sugar
2 cups tomato juice, fresh or canned	6 to 6½ cups all-purpose flour, unsifted

1. Combine yeast, ¼ cup warm water, and ¼ teaspoon sugar in a small bowl. Let sit until foamy, about 10 minutes.
2. Heat tomato juice and butter in a saucepan just until warm. Butter does not have to melt.
3. In a large bowl combine salt, 2 tablespoons sugar, and 2 cups of the flour. Blend well.
4. Add tomato juice mixture and yeast mixture to flour mixture and beat fifty strokes with a wire whisk or rotary beater.
5. Add another ½ cup flour to mixture and beat another fifty strokes.
6. With a wooden spoon gradually stir in remaining flour, ½ cupful at a time, to make a stiff dough. Dough is ready when it begins to pull away from the sides of the bowl. Don't add more flour than necessary.
7. Turn dough out on a floured surface and knead, adding more flour only as needed, until dough is smooth and satiny—about 10 minutes.
8. Put dough in a greased bowl, turning once to grease top. Cover bowl with a towel and set in a warm place (about 80°F.) to rise until doubled in bulk. Takes about 1½ hours.
9. Punch down; turn out onto floured board and knead slightly to remove air bubbles.
10. Divide into two portions. Shape into smooth ovals—pinch bottom seam, turn ends under, and seal.
11. Put loaves in lightly greased pans, seam side down. Cover and let rise again in a warm place until almost doubled (about 45 minutes).
12. Bake in 350°F. oven about 45 minutes until nicely browned. Remove from pans and cool on wire racks. Makes two loaves.

Tomato breads offer unusual, beguiling flavors. From left to right: tomato bread; tomato herb bread; tomato caraway buffet loaf; and tomato egg braid.

Tomato egg braid

Follow directions for tomato bread but use 1¾ cups tomato juice. After adding the ½ cup flour (step 5), add two beaten eggs and beat an additional fifty strokes, or until well blended. Again, follow the tomato bread instructions.

Divide the dough for both loaves into three equal parts and roll them into strands about 14 inches long. Braid each trio of strands together, pinching ends to seal.

Let rise on lightly greased baking sheets until almost doubled in bulk (about 45 minutes). Brush with slightly beaten egg before baking. Bake at 350°F. for 30 to 35 minutes until nicely browned.

Tomato caraway buffet loaves

Follow directions for tomato bread, adding 1 tablespoon caraway seed to the dry ingredients.

After the first rising, divide the dough into four equal parts and roll each into long, thin loaves about 12 to 14 inches long. Let rise on lightly greased baking sheets until almost doubled in bulk (35 to 45 minutes).

Brush with slightly beaten egg and sprinkle with more caraway seeds before baking. Bake at 350°F. until lightly browned, about 30 minutes. Makes four loaves.

Fresh tomato pizza

Pizza in our home is usually served as a first course, or with the antipasto. It is made with a basic white bread dough and shaped on a baking sheet. The topping consists of fresh sliced tomatoes, anchovy fillets, and cheese. For a main course add toppings of your own choice—thin-sliced salami, minced ham, shrimp, olives, ground beef, or sausage.

Dough

¼ teaspoon sugar	1½ cups all-purpose flour
¼ cup warm water (105–115°F.)	1 teaspoon salt
1½ teaspoons dry yeast	1 tablespoon butter

1. Dissolve sugar in warm water and sprinkle yeast on top. Set aside for 10 minutes, or until foamy.
2. Sift flour and salt into a bowl. With pastry blender cut in butter until well blended.
3. Add yeast mixture to flour and mix to a dough. Add more flour if dough is sticky.
4. Turn out onto floured surface and knead until smooth and elastic, about 10 minutes.
5. Put into oiled bowl; turn once to coat all sides. Cover and let rise in a warm place (80°F.) until doubled in bulk.
6. Punch down; turn out onto floured board and knead slightly to remove air bubbles.
7. Roll into a circle ¼ inch thick and 12 inches wide. Place on oiled baking sheet.

Topping

Olive oil	4 medium tomatoes, peeled and sliced
Salt and pepper	
4 ounces mozzarella cheese, thinly sliced or shredded	12 anchovy fillets
	Oregano

1. Brush top of dough base lightly with olive oil. Sprinkle with salt and pepper.
2. Arrange cheese and tomato slices over dough. Lay anchovy fillets between tomato slices. Sprinkle generously with oregano.
3. Bake in 450°F. oven about 20 minutes until crust is golden brown. Serves six as an appetizer, or two as a main course.

Fresh tomato pizza boasts a chewy crust and vine-ripened tomatoes.

Tomato herb bread

Besides being very tasty, this bread is pretty to look at, with specks of red and green blended through it. I like to use it for cheese or cold breast-of-chicken sandwiches. It can be baked in a variety of pans—loaf pans, 9-inch pie plates or cake pans, or 2-quart casserole or soufflé dishes.

1 package active dry yeast	2 eggs, beaten
¼ cup warm water (105–115°F.)	1 tablespoon dried onion flakes
¼ teaspoon sugar	1 large tomato, peeled, seeded, and chopped
1½ cups milk	1 teaspoon dried basil
3 tablespoons butter	¼ teaspoon marjoram
2 teaspoons salt	¼ teaspoon thyme
2 tablespoons sugar	
5½ to 6 cups all-purpose flour, unsifted	

1. In a small bowl combine yeast, warm water, and ¼ teaspoon sugar. Let sit until foamy, about 10 minutes.
2. Heat milk and butter in a saucepan just until warm. Butter does not have to melt.
3. In a large bowl combine salt, 2 tablespoons sugar and 2 cups of the flour. Blend well.
4. Add milk mixture to flour mixture and beat fifty strokes with a wire whisk or rotary beater.
5. Add yeast mixture and another ½ cup flour and beat another fifty strokes.
6. Add beaten eggs and beat mixture until thoroughly blended.
7. Add dried onion flakes, tomato, and herbs. Blend well.
8. With a wooden spoon stir in remaining flour, ½ cup at a time, only until mixture becomes a stiff dough and starts to pull away from the sides of the bowl. Don't add more flour than necessary.
9. Turn dough out on a floured surface and knead, adding more flour only as it is needed, until dough is smooth and satiny—about 10 minutes.
10. Put dough in a greased bowl, turning once to grease top. Cover bowl with a towel and set in a warm place (about 80°F.) to rise until doubled. Takes about 1½ hours.
11. Punch down; turn out onto floured board and knead slightly to remove air bubbles.
12. Divide into two portions. Shape into ovals or rounds.
13. Put loaves in lightly greased pans. Cover and let rise again in warm place until almost doubled (about 45 minutes).
14. Bake in 350°F. oven about 35 to 45 minutes, depending upon the size of the pan. Loaves will look nicely browned and start to pull away from the sides of the pan when they are done.
15. Remove from pans and cool on wire racks. Makes two loaves.

Desserts made with green tomatoes include (clockwise from bottom): green tomato pie; mock date bars; and mystery fudge cake.

Desserts

The green tomato plays a surprising part in the following three recipes.

Green tomato pie

This pie is often compared to rhubarb or tart green apple pie. Actually, it has a flavor all its own. I like to serve it slightly warmed, with a scoop of vanilla ice cream. Use your favorite pastry recipe. A flaky, tender pie crust is best with any fruit pie.

Filling

6 cups sliced green tomatoes	Small pinch ground cloves
Boiling water	Grated rind and juice
1 cup sugar	of 1 lemon
¼ teaspoon salt	2 tablespoons butter or
3 tablespoons flour	margarine
¼ teaspoon ground nutmeg	Pastry for 2-crust 9-inch pie
¼ teaspoon cinnamon	

1. Wash tomatoes; do not peel. Slice ⅛ inch thick into bowl. Pour on boiling water to cover; let stand 3 minutes. Drain.
2. In a small bowl combine sugar, salt, flour, and spices. Combine lemon juice and rind in another bowl.
3. Fill pastry-lined pie dish with layers of green tomatoes, sprinkling each layer with sugar mixture, dots of butter, and small amounts of lemon mixture.
4. When pan is filled, arrange pastry strips in a lattice pattern over filling. Moisten edges to seal and flute or press together with a fork.
5. Bake in preheated 450°F. oven for 8 to 10 minutes. Then reduce heat to 375°F. and bake until tomatoes are tender, about 40 minutes.
6. Remove to a wire rack to cool.

Mystery fudge cake

This really delicious chocolate fudge cake is about the moistest I have ever tasted. It keeps for days in the refrigerator, without losing its freshness. The mystery: green tomatoes! Sounds strange, I know, but when the tomatoes are blended with all the other ingredients, there is absolutely no way one can detect the secret ingredient.

2½ cups regular, all-purpose flour	3 eggs
½ cup cocoa	2 teaspoons vanilla
2½ teaspoons baking powder	2 teaspoons grated orange peel
2 teaspoons baking soda	2 cups coarsely grated green tomato
1 teaspoon salt	
1 teaspoon cinnamon	1 cup finely chopped walnuts
¾ cup butter or margarine	½ cup milk
2 cups sugar	

1. Combine dry ingredients in a large bowl and set aside.
2. In another bowl beat together butter and sugar until smooth.
3. Add eggs one at a time and beat well after each addition.
4. With a wooden spoon, stir in vanilla, orange peel, and green tomatoes.
5. Stir the nuts into the sifted dry ingredients and add to tomato mixture alternately with milk.
6. Pour batter into a greased and floured 10-inch tube or Bundt pan.
7. Bake at 350°F. until a wooden pick inserted in center comes out clean, about 1 hour.
8. Cool in pan 15 minutes, then turn out onto a wire rack and cool.
9. Sprinkle with powdered sugar before serving.

Mock date bars

This delightfully chewy bar-type cookie is also very economical since it doesn't use dates at all. The filling is made with ground green tomatoes and walnuts, but I doubt if anyone would ever know the difference. The whole-wheat flour makes it extra wholesome and gives it a nutlike flavor.

Filling

2 cups ground green tomatoes	1 teaspoon cinnamon
½ cup plus 2 tablespoons sugar	¼ teaspoon cloves
Juice and grated peel of 1 orange	½ teaspoon salt
1 tablespoon lemon juice	½ cup chopped walnuts

1. Combine all above ingredients, except walnuts, in a saucepan and cook until most of liquid has evaporated and mixture is quite thick. Stir occasionally.
2. Stir in walnuts and cool while preparing crust.

Crust

½ cup butter or margarine	1 teaspoon baking powder
1 cup firmly packed brown sugar	½ teaspoon baking soda
2 teaspoons vanilla	1 teaspoon salt
1½ cups sifted whole-wheat flour	1 cup quick-cooking oatmeal

1. Cream butter, brown sugar, and vanilla together.
2. Sift together whole-wheat flour, baking powder, baking soda, and salt. Stir into creamed mixture until smooth.
3. Add oatmeal and blend thoroughly.
4. Grease and flour an 8 × 12-inch baking pan. Press half of the mixture firmly into pan. Cover with filling.
5. Place remaining oatmeal mixture over filling. Press down.
6. Bake at 350°F. for 30 minutes. Cool. Cut into 2-inch squares. Makes 24.

Canning Tomatoes

I welcome what other people might consider an overabundance of tomatoes. A large crop means enough canned tomatoes to see me through the rest of the year. I'll match my canned tomatoes with any you can buy in the store.

I use two methods of canning tomatoes: the cold-pack method, and the hot-pack. The difference is this: cold-pack tomatoes are peeled, dropped into the jars whole, and processed. They retain their shape after canning. Hot-pack tomatoes are packed into the jars hot; that is, they are peeled, quartered, heated to the boiling point, and then packed into the jars. The result is more like a sauce.

Equipment needed

☐ Canning jars. (I find the wide-mouth quart size the most practical.)
☐ Metal rings and lids to fit the jars. (New lids must be used for each canning. Rings may be reused as long as they are in good condition and free from rust.)
☐ Water-bath canner with a metal rack inside to hold the jars, and a tight-fitting cover, or any large kettle that is deep enough to permit water to cover the jars at least 1 inch over the tops, with a little extra space to allow for boiling. You can improvise a rack with strips of wood or wire, or use any size rack that will allow the boiling water to circulate under the jars.
☐ Jar lifter, designed to wrap around jars while filling, and to grasp neck of jars when lifting in and out of the boiling water.
☐ Miscellaneous utensils: Canning funnel, paring knife, long knife or narrow spatula, clean cloth, plastic or wooden spoon, clock or kitchen timer, measuring spoons, towels, or cooling rack.

The ingredients. The ingredients are simple: tomatoes and a little salt. Select the tomatoes carefully. Use only fresh, firm, ripe tomatoes, free from any decayed spots. After the jars are filled with tomatoes, add salt at the rate of ½ teaspoon per pint, or 1 teaspoon per quart, depending on the size jars you use.

Preparation

1. Set out all equipment and utensils within easy reach. Fill kettle two-thirds full with water and put on high heat to boil. Keep a teakettle filled with hot water, which will be needed later when all the jars are filled and sealed.
2. Examine tops of jars to make sure they have no nicks, cracks, or sharp edges that would prevent a perfect seal. Imperfect jars should not be used for canning.
3. Wash the jars thoroughly in hot, soapy water. Rinse completely. Keep jars in hot water until you are ready to use them.
4. Select enough tomatoes to make one canner load—most canners hold seven jars. It takes approximately 2½ to 3 pounds of tomatoes for each quart jar.
5. Peel tomatoes according to directions on page 68. Cut out core, remove or trim away any green spots.

Above: Scald lids with hot water. This softens their sealing compound.

Left: Canning equipment (clockwise from top): steam pressure canner, jelly bag and stand, large measuring cup, scale, colander, jar lifter, long-handled spoons, vegetable brush, ladles, thermometer, cooling rack, labels, cheesecloth, knives, measuring cups, timer, food mill, water-bath canning rack and jars, wide-mouth funnel, and water-bath canner.

Cold Pack Tomatoes

Boil containers for 15 minutes to sterilize.

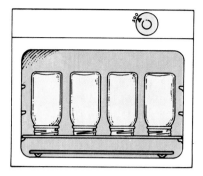

Set jars in a 200°F oven to dry and keep them hot.

Fill jars.

Headspace

Screw on ring bands to hold lids in place. Handle hot jars with rubber gloves to protect hands.

Lift jars straight up to avoid tipping contents.

Test for a seal by pressing the center of the lid gently; it should be drawn down slightly. If it bounces up and down to the pressure of your finger, the jar is *not* properly sealed.

To cold-pack tomatoes

1. Remove one jar from water and drain. Place funnel on jar. Drop whole tomatoes into jar. Cut very large tomatoes into quarters, if necessary.
2. Remove funnel and press tomatoes gently to fill space, to within ½ inch of the top of the jars. To get the proper headspace, add a little more tomato, or pour off a little juice. Do not add water.
3. Add 1 teaspoon salt to each quart jar, or ½ teaspoon to each pint.
4. Run a long knife or narrow spatula between tomatoes and jar to release any trapped air bubbles.
5. Wipe the top of the jar with a clean, damp cloth and check that no seeds or bits of tomato are clinging to the rim or outer threads.
6. Remove one lid from the boiling water and place it flat on top of the jar, with the sealing compound next to the glass. Place metal ring over lid and screw it down *firmly*.
7. When all jars are filled, stand them on the rack in the canner. Water should cover jars by at least 1 inch. Add more water (from the teakettle) if necessary.

8. Put cover on canner. Bring water to a rolling boil. Begin counting processing time—45 minutes for quarts; 35 minutes for pints. Reduce water to hard simmer and hold it there the entire time.
9. Using the jar lifter, remove jars from the canner and set on a rack or folded cloth, allowing space between jars for air circulation. Do not set jars in a draft or cover them. Do not tighten metal rings.
10. When jars are completely cool (about 12 hours), test for seal by pressing down on the center of the lid. If the dome is down and gives out a clear, ringing sound when tapped with a spoon, the jar is sealed. Remove bands and store jars in a cool, dark, dry place.

To hot-pack tomatoes. Peel and quarter tomatoes. Put in large pan and heat slowly to the boiling point. Stir frequently to avoid scorching. Fill jars while tomatoes are still hot.

Follow the procedure for cold-pack tomatoes with the following change: Subtract 10 minutes from the processing time, for both quarts and pints.

Both red and green tomatoes are used for jams, marmalades, preserves, and butter.

Jams, Butter, Marmalade, and Preserves

In spring, when planning our vegetable garden, we have no worry about overplanting tomatoes. I always make sure we plant enough so that I'll have a good crop of both red and green tomatoes to put up the jams, marmalade, and other good things my family enjoys so much.

Red tomato jam

This beautifully clear, red jam uses many of the fully or over-ripe tomatoes. I always make this toward the end of the season when tomatoes are ripening quicker than I can use them fresh.

3 pounds (6 large) fully ripe tomatoes	1 box (2½ ounces) powdered fruit pectin
1 lemon, thinly sliced	4 cups sugar

1. Scald, peel, and quarter tomatoes, removing stems and cores. Remove seeds and drain off juice, reserving only the pulp.
2. Bring to boil in a large kettle. Reduce heat and simmer, uncovered, for 8 to 10 minutes. Measure; there should be 3 cups.
3. Put tomatoes, lemon, and pectin in a large kettle. Bring to a full boil, stirring constantly. Add sugar and boil rapidly for another 2 minutes.
4. Cook for 5 minutes, stirring occasionally.
5. Fill sterilized jars and seal. Process in boiling-water bath for 10 minutes. (See pages 104 and 105.) Makes 2 pints.

Green tomato mincemeat

I can hardly wait for my green tomatoes to get large enough so that I can make this marvelous mincemeat. Although it requires 3 hours of simmering and must be stirred often, it is not as difficult to make as the time involved would suggest. It is well worth the time spent. I use it in cookies, cakes, and pies, or warmed and served over vanilla ice cream. A bit of rum or brandy added to the warmed mincemeat gives it a nice festive touch and a delicate but distinctive flavor.

6 cups chopped, peeled apples	1 teaspoon ground cloves
6 cups chopped, green tomatoes	¾ teaspoon allspice
4 cups light brown sugar	¾ teaspoon mace
1¼ cups cider vinegar	2 teaspoons salt
2 cups golden raisins	½ teaspoon freshly ground black pepper
3 teaspoons cinnamon	½ cup butter

1. Mix the apples and tomatoes together. Add the remaining ingredients except the butter.
2. Bring gradually to a boil, in a large pot, and simmer for 3 hours, stirring often.
3. Add the butter and mix well. Spoon into hot, sterilized, canning jars and seal.
4. Process in boiling-water bath for 25 minutes. (See pages 104 and 105.)
5. Remove from kettle and allow to cool.
6. Store in a cool, dark, dry place. Makes about 5 pints.

Green tomato-citrus marmalade

This marmalade is our favorite because it is not quite as sweet as most. The green tomatoes soften considerably after cooking and the jam becomes very thick. Remember to stir constantly, as it thickens rapidly once it comes to a full boil.

1½ quarts green tomatoes, thinly sliced.	½ teaspoon salt
3 cups sugar	2 lemons
	2 oranges

1. Mix tomatoes, sugar, and salt in a large bowl.
2. Peel lemons and oranges. Boil peel for 8 minutes in enough water to cover. Drain off and discard the water. Cut peel into thin strips.
3. Slice lemon and orange pulp very thin and remove seeds.
4. Combine peel, citrus pulp, and tomato mixture in a large kettle. Heat to boiling and cook rapidly, stirring constantly until thickened, about 45 minutes.
5. Pour into sterilized jars and seal. Process in boiling water bath for 10 minutes. (See pages 104 and 105.) Makes 2 pints.

Green tomato jam

I make this jam early in the season. Pick the tomatoes when they are of a good size and about a week before they will turn red.

6 cups (about 2½ pounds) chopped green tomatoes	4 cups sugar
Hot water	2 lemons, thinly sliced

1. Cover tomatoes with hot water and boil for 5 minutes.
2. Drain and add sugar. Let stand for 3 hours or longer.
3. Drain syrup into kettle; bring to a boil and cook rapidly until quite thick.
4. Add tomatoes and sliced lemon and cook until thick and clear, about 10 minutes.
5. Pack into sterilized jars and seal. (See pages 104 and 105.) Makes 2 pints.

Tomato-apple butter

Tomatoes and apples combine to make a very tasty butter. It's delicious on homemade biscuits and very good in peanut butter sandwiches.

3 pounds (about 6) ripe tomatoes	1½ teaspoons cinnamon
3 green apples	½ teaspoon ground cloves
2 tablespoons lemon juice	¼ teaspoon allspice
1 teaspoon salt	¼ teaspoon nutmeg
	2½ cups brown sugar

1. Scald, peel, and quarter tomatoes. Cook, covered, until mushy, stirring occasionally. Press through a sieve to remove any seeds. Measure; there should be about 4 cups.
2. Peel, core, and quarter apples. Cook in ½ cup water until mushy, about 15 minutes.
3. Combine tomato purée and apple pulp in a large kettle. Add remaining ingredients. Bring to a boil and simmer, uncovered, stirring frequently for 45 minutes, or until thick.
4. Fill sterilized jars and seal. Process in boiling-water bath for 10 minutes. (See pages 104 and 105.) Makes 2 pints.

Piccalilli

1 quart cabbage, chopped	1 stick (2 inches) cinnamon
1 quart chopped green tomatoes	1 teaspoon *each* whole cloves and whole allspice
1 cup chopped celery	1½ cups cider vinegar
2 large onions, chopped	1½ cups water
2 sweet red peppers, seeded and chopped	2 cups brown sugar, firmly packed
2 green peppers, seeded and chopped	1 teaspoon dry mustard
¼ cup salt	1 teaspoon turmeric
	Dash hot pepper sauce

1. Combine vegetables and salt; cover and let stand overnight.
2. Drain off as much liquid as possible, pressing through a clean, thin white cloth, if necessary.
3. Place cinnamon, cloves, and allspice in a cheesecloth bag.
4. Place vegetables, spice bag, vinegar, water, sugar, dry mustard, turmeric, and hot pepper sauce in a large kettle.
5. Bring to the boiling point; reduce heat and simmer for 20 minutes.
6. Pour into sterilized jars and seal. Process in boiling-water bath 5 minutes. (See pages 104 and 105.) Makes 6 pints.

Piccalilli makes good use of garden vegetables and goes wonderfully with hamburgers and hot dogs.

Green tomato relish

2 cups (4 or 5 medium) ground green tomatoes
2 cups (2 medium) peeled and ground cucumbers
2 cups (4 medium) ground onions
3 medium-size tart apples, peeled and ground
1 green pepper, seeded and ground
2 small, sweet red peppers, seeded and ground
4 cups water
1½ tablespoons salt
2 cups white sugar
2 cups cider vinegar
1 tablespoon mustard seed
6 tablespoons all-purpose flour
1 tablespoon dry mustard
¼ teaspoon turmeric

1. Mix tomatoes, cucumbers, onions, apples, peppers, water, and salt in a large kettle. Let stand for 24 hours; drain off liquid.
2. Add sugar, 1½ cups of the vinegar, and mustard seed. Bring to a slow boil and cook for 30 minutes, stirring occasionally.
3. Make a paste of flour, dry mustard, turmeric, and remaining ½ cup vinegar. Stir into boiling mixture.
4. Simmer for additional 30 minutes or until mixture has thickened, stirring occasionally.
5. Fill sterilized jars and seal. Process in boiling-water bath for 10 minutes. (See pages 104 and 105.) Makes 4 pints.

Tomatoes—whether ripe or green, mature or miniature—can be turned into a variety of relishes and condiments.

Canning preserves your crop for use after the season is over, but follow the proper safety procedures to ensure the health of yourself and your family.

About Safety

As Annette Fabri wrote her instructions for canning, much talk and a very thorough investigation was going on about the safety factor in canning tomatoes.

The U.S.D.A., with well-documented facts, is attempting to disprove the false rumors and clear up old myths.

The rumors have swirled about the acidity of tomatoes and dangers in canning them. You may have heard them: "You can be poisoned by home-canned tomatoes." "Many of the newly introduced varieties are too low in acidity to can in the usual way." "All California varieties are lower in acidity than Eastern varieties." "The small tomatoes should not be used in canning."

Preventing botulism. G. M. Sapers of the U.S.D.A. at the Eastern Regional Research Center in Philadelphia, Pennsylvania, discusses these attitudes.

"Considerable concern has been expressed by the public over the risk of botulism from home-canned tomatoes. This has been engendered in part by recent magazine articles and news items, some of which unfortunately contain inaccurate and misleading information. It has been stated, for example, that 'new strains of tomatoes,' including 'pale yellow-orange tomatoes as well as small cherry or patio ones,' contain insufficient acid to prevent the growth of *Clostridium botulinum*. Such statements may also imply that the consumer of home-canned tomatoes faces a significant danger.

"The seriousness of botulism should never be understated. However, we believe that the risk to home canners of tomatoes is very small. Data compiled by the Center for Disease Control, U.S. Department of Health, Education, and Welfare, show only a handful of cases of botulism due to home-canned tomatoes in recent years, none fatal. Furthermore, these documented cases were not associated with low-acid tomatoes."

The U.S.D.A. has collected data on 356 tomato cultivars from reports from every region in the United States. These reports were in addition to the department's continuing study of varieties at Doylestown, Pennsylvania, and Beltsville, Maryland. From these data we quote the pH readings given in the accompanying chart.

The U.S.D.A. is continuing to study the safety factors related to individual cultivars, as well as the effect of various methods of acidulation. The U.S.D.A. concludes that:

"The home canner should not be overly concerned about hazards associated with the selection of specific tomato varieties for home canning. It is far more important for the home canner to select tomatoes that are not over-ripe, to follow the recommendations of reliable canning guides explicitly, and to destroy (without tasting) any home-canned product that appears abnormal in any way. We especially recommend that the home canner obtain Home and Garden Bulletin No. 8, *Home Canning of Fruits and Vegetables*, which is available for 45¢ from the Superintendent of Documents, U.S. Government Printing Office, Washington, DC 20402."

What is pH? The following definition of pH is from Webster's New Collegiate Dictionary:

"pH: The negative logarithm of the effective hydrogen-ion concentration of hydrogen-ion activity in gram equivalents per liter used in expressing both acidity and alkalinity on a scale whose values run from 0 to 14 with 7 representing neutrality, numbers less than 7 increasing acidity, and numbers greater than 7 increasing alkalinity; also, the condition represented by such a number."

Note carefully that the definition says, "numbers less than 7 increasing acidity, and numbers greater than 7 increasing alkalinity." In other words, when you say it has a high acidity, it has a low pH, and when it has a high alkalinity, it has a high pH.

Two measurements of acidity are used for tomatoes: "titratable acidity," and "pH."

Here is the chart of pH values for various foods:

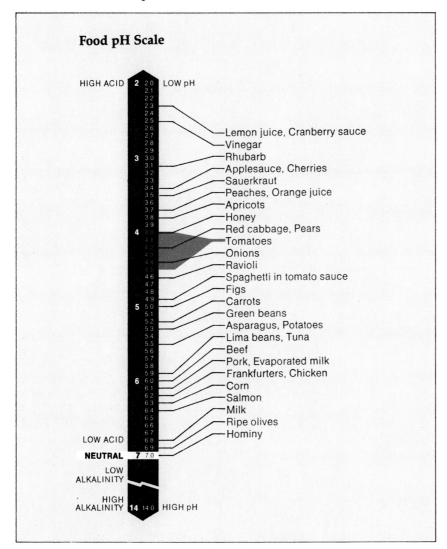

Food pH Scale

HIGH ACID **2** 2.0 LOW pH

Lemon juice, Cranberry sauce
Vinegar
3 Rhubarb
Applesauce, Cherries
Sauerkraut
Peaches, Orange juice
Apricots
Honey
Red cabbage, Pears
4 Tomatoes
Onions
Ravioli
Spaghetti in tomato sauce
Figs
Carrots
5 Green beans
Asparagus, Potatoes
Lima beans, Tuna
Beef
Pork, Evaporated milk
Frankfurters, Chicken
6 Corn
Salmon
Milk
Ripe olives
Hominy

LOW ACID
NEUTRAL **7** 7.0
LOW ALKALINITY
HIGH ALKALINITY **14** 14.0 HIGH pH

Adding acid. For insurance that the tomatoes you can are in the low pH range, add ¼ teaspoon citric acid or 1 tablespoon lemon juice per pint of tomato product.

The chart below shows what happens to the pH ratings of various tomato cultivars when different acids are added. Note that the pH is not significantly lowered by the addition of 1 teaspoon lemon juice per pint.

Tomato Variety	Original pH	pH after adding ¼ tsp. citric acid per pint	pH after adding 1 tsp. lemon juice per pint	pH after adding 1 tbsp. lemon juice per pint
'Ace'	4.4	4.1	4.3	4.2
'Ace 55 VF'	4.6	4.2	4.5	4.3
'Big Early'	4.4	4.0	4.3	4.1
'Big Girl'	4.5	4.1	4.4	4.2
'Garden State'	4.5	4.2	4.4	4.3
'Valiant'	4.4	3.9	4.3	4.1

Top: The various shapes of tomatoes. From left to right: globe, deep globe, oblate, and deep oblate. Center: The interior structure—the ratio of meat to gel—also varies. Bottom: The size, too, varies, whether measured in inches or ounces.

TOMATO VARIETIES

Varieties of the tomato abound— more than a hundred are listed here. But new types are as inevitable as the differences in regional climate and soil and local preference.

This chapter contains descriptions and photographs of many tomato varieties. In botanical terms, these varieties should technically be referred to as cultivars—cultivated varieties—to indicate that they have been cultivated, as opposed to simple varieties, which occur naturally. For the convenience of the home gardener, however, they are generally referred to as varieties. To help the home gardener with a particular interest, the variety descriptions have been divided into fourteen different categories.

Planting times should be adjusted according to climatic conditions to take advantage of the warm growing season in which tomatoes most thrive. Early and Midseason varieties are therefore most appropriate for regions with short growing seasons. In areas with an extended growing season, the Late Season varieties may also be successful.

Almost all of the variety descriptions are presented in the same format. Please note that the entries are listed in order of ripening, and *not* in alphabetical order. Reading from left to right across the page, you will find the following information:

First, there is an illustration of the shape of the particular variety. Tomatoes, except for paste tomatoes, are classified in these basic shapes. (For the shape of paste tomatoes, see page 129.)

The illustratons of shape do not vary according to actual size. The relative size of the variety is noted in the description column on the right.

Following the illustration, the name of the variety appears. Directly after the name, a statement in parentheses will tell you if the variety is a hybrid, which will not breed true from seed.

Under the name of the variety you will find the word "Determinate" or "Indeterminate," which indicates how the plant grows and how it should be trained in the garden. For definitions of these terms, see pages 14, 15, and 16.

Below this information you can check to see whether or not the variety is resistant to any of the common tomato diseases. If a variety is resistant to a particular disease such as verticillium wilt (V), fusarium wilt (F), or nematodes (N), the disease will be noted. If there are no diseases listed, the variety is not resistant to these diseases.

In the next column (Region) a small map with a shaded area or areas indicates where the variety is best adapted.

This map is meant as a general growing guide. Beginning on page 130 tomato varieties have been grouped by region. These varieties are particularly suited to certain localized conditions. Therefore, the map that accompanies these entries is shaded in more specific areas. For instance, a particular state may be shaded.

The third column (Transplant to Harvest) indicates the number of days it takes to produce the first tomatoes from the time a transplant is planted in the garden or greenhouse. This is a relative figure that is sure to differ

Globe   Deep   Oblate   Deep
         globe   oblate

from garden to garden. The actual number of days it takes a particular variety to produce a crop in your own garden will depend upon the weather, season, date of transplant, and soil temperature. Use this number as a rough guide only.

The fourth column (Description) gives the origin, growth habits, and cultural requirements of the individual varieties. In this column the clues provided will help set each variety apart from scores of similar varieties. Also, a number of varieties are endorsed as worthy of a trial in your garden. Those judgments are based on reports from trials in various areas, and on the recommendations of the Extension Service.

A variety is described as "widely adapted" when its performance rates high in many varied climates. Gardeners in climates too cold or too hot or with a short growing season should first favor the local variety recommendation, and then the widely adapted varieties. Local recommendations are set apart under the headings of "Regional Specials."

At the end of the description, availability is indicated by a *number code*. Varieties are available as seeds from mail-order seed companies, as small plants at garden stores, in seed stores, or in seed display racks.

On pages 139 and 140 you will find a list of seed companies. Each has been given a number. If a variety is noted as "widely available," it is available in more than eight catalogs. If a variety is available in fewer than eight catalogs, the number of the seed company (or companies) that carries the item is listed following the description of the variety. For example: 'Redpak', Available: (13).

By checking the catalog listings on page 139, you will find that (13) is the Joseph Harris Co.

Early Season Varieties

Shape, Name, and Disease Resistance	Region Best Adapted	Transplant to Harvest	Description
'Rocket' (Standard) Determinate		50 days	Tomatoes produced by 'Rocket' are small in size (3 to 4 oz.) and medium firm. The variety was developed by the Canadian Department of Agriculture specifically for areas with short growing seasons. The small vines are ideal for container growing. Available: (27), (38), (40), (41), (42).
'Sweet-N-Early' (Hybrid) Indeterminate Verticillium wilt Fusarium wilt		55 days	'Sweet-N-Early' is similar to 'Sweet 100' (see page 115) except that the tomatoes are larger (3 to 4 oz.) and they are not as sweet. The vines bear clusters of fruit in prolific quantities. Available: (53).
'Starfire' (Standard) Determinate		56 days	'Starfire' is an improved version of 'Fireball' (see page 116) developed by the Canadian Department of Agriculture at Morden, Manitoba. It has better foliage cover than its predecessor and medium-large (6 oz.) fruits on a compact, bushy vine. Widely available.
'Ultra Girl' (Hybrid) Semideterminate Verticillium wilt Fusarium wilt Nematodes		56 days	This triple disease-resistant hybrid was developed by the Stokes Seed Co. The fruit is medium-large (8 to 9 oz.) with good resistance to cracking. Available: (27).
'Earliana – 498' (Standard) Indeterminate		58 days	This old-time favorite ripens early in the season. Fruits are medium-size (5 to 6 oz.) and the vines provide good foliage cover. 'Earliana' is recommended by Agricultural Extension Services (A.E.S.) in Colorado, Idaho, Montana, and Nevada. Widely available.

Shape, Name, and Disease Resistance	Region Best Adapted	Transplant to Harvest	Description
'Manitoba' (Standard) Determinate		60 days	This variety was developed by the Canada Agricultural Experimental Farms at Morden, Manitoba. It is similar to 'Bush Beefsteak' (see page 124) but has smoother, medium-size (6 to 7 oz.) fruit. The vines are compact, with medium foliage cover. Available: (27), (38), (41), (42).
'Jetfire' (Hybrid) Determinate Verticillium wilt Fusarium wilt		60 days	'Jetfire' produces slightly larger and firmer fruit than 'Springset' (see page 116). The vines also provide better foliage cover. Available: (27).
'Scotia' (Standard) Determinate		60 days	A productive tomato that sets well in cool weather. 'Scotia' was developed by the Dominion Experimental Farm in Nova Scotia, Canada. The fruits are small (4 oz.) but plentiful. Available: (27), (38), (41), (42).
'Hasty Boy' (Hybrid) Indeterminate Verticillium wilt Fusarium wilt		60 days	A medium-size, crack-resistant, meaty tomato. For an early variety 'Hasty Boy' is very prolific. Available: (15).
'Early Cascade' (Hybrid) Indeterminate Verticillium wilt Fusarium wilt		61 days	'Early Cascade' is a very early and very tall cascading type of tomato plant developed by the Petoseed Co. The medium-size tomatoes are good tasting and are produced in abundance. Widely available.
'Quebec #13' (Standard) Determinate		62 days	'Quebec' tomatoes are deep red, very firm, and of medium size (5 to 6 oz.). The "Beefsteak"-type fruits are excellent for canning. Available: (27), (38), (40).
'Early Girl' (Hybrid) Indeterminate Verticillium wilt		62 days	This variety, developed by the George Ball Co., produces high yields of firm, smooth, meaty, medium-size (4 to 5 oz.) fruits. 'Early Girl' bears both early and late in the season and is resistant to cracking. The vines are sturdy, with good foliage protection against sunscald, and they can be staked or grown in cages. Plants often available at nurseries. Available: (5), (30).
'Burpee's Big Early' (Hybrid) Indeterminate		62 days	'Burpee's Big Early' is noteworthy for its early production of large, thick-walled fruit. Originated by the Burpee Seed Co., this rugged hybrid produces a vigorous vine with heavy foliage. Can be grown in a trellis or cage. Available: (5), (27).
'Sweet 100' (Hybrid) Indeterminate		62 days	'Sweet 100' is an unusual and worthwhile tomato. It produces large, multiple-branched clusters of very sweet 1-inch fruits, with twenty or more fruits per cluster. The vine itself is vigorous, with narrow leaves. The originator, Goldsmith Seed, Inc., recommends pruning the plants to one stem and growing with a stake or in a cage. Available: (5), (18), (21), (28), (36), (41).

Early Season Varieties (continued)

Shape, Name, and Disease Resistance	Region Best Adapted	Transplant to Harvest	Description
'Gardener' (Hybrid) Indeterminate Verticillium wilt Fusarium wilt		63 days	This hybrid, developed by Cornell University, is well adapted to the Northeast region. Its medium-size fruits (6 oz.) are firm and crack-resistant. The vine produces medium foliage cover, and should be grown staked, on a trellis or in a cage. Available: (27), (43).
'New Yorker' (Standard) Determinate Verticillium wilt		64 days	'New Yorker' is widely recommended for planting as an early variety before the main crop. The small, very compact vines produce a concentrated harvest (only about 10 days) of medium-size fruits (6 oz.); after that, the fruit size decreases dramatically. 'New Yorker' is similar to 'Fireball' (see below) but with far better foliage cover. Widely available.
'Fireball' (Standard) Determinate		64 days	Originated by the Harris Seed Co., 'Fireball' was bred for early production. The vines are short, compact, and have sparse foliage. To avoid sunscald this variety should be grown in a cage. The fruits are medium-size (4 to 5 oz.), firm, and are produced during a short, concentrated harvest season. Recommended by Agricultural Extension Services in Minnesota, Idaho, Wyoming, and Montana. Widely available.
'Spring Giant' (Hybrid) Determinate Vericillium wilt Fusarium wilt Nematodes		65 days	This 1967 All-America Selection (the first tomato to win this award) was originated by the Dessert Seed Co. 'Spring Giant' is a high-yielding variety; its fruits have thick walls and a small core. It produces an early crop in a concentrated harvest season. The plant offers little sunscald protection and is therefore best grown in a short cage. Widely available.
'Early Boy' (Hybrid) Determinate		65 days	Another tomato originated by the Dessert Seed Co., 'Early Boy' produces deep scarlet, smooth-skinned, large (7 to 9 oz.) fruit. The tomatoes are firm-fleshed, thick-walled, and free from white cores. The plant is a strong-growing determinate with dark green foliage. Available: (2).
'Springset' (Hybrid) Determinate Verticillium wilt Fusarium wilt		65 days	Petoseed Co. developed this variety, which produces a high yield of medium-size (5 to 6 oz.) firm fruit over a short, concentrated harvest season. The fruit is quite crack-resistant. Although the vine is vigorous, it is open and offers little sunscald protection unless grown in a cage or on a short trellis. Widely available.

Early ripening 'Sweet 100' bears clusters of cherry-sized fruit.

'Early Girl'

'Big Early'

'New Yorker'

'Spring Giant'

'Springset'

Midseason Varieties

Shape, Name, and Disease Resistance	Region Best Adapted	Transplant to Harvest	Description
'Sunripe' (Hybrid) Determinate Verticillium wilt Fusarium wilt Nematodes		69 days	Originated by the George Ball Co., 'Sunripe' has a strong vine that produces very large fruit resistant to cracking. The plant can be trained on a short stake or grown in wire cages. Widely available.
'Basket Vee' (Standard) Small determinate Verticillium wilt		70 days	A deep red, meaty, crack-resistant variety. The fact that this tomato is very firm makes it an excellent canner. Available: (27).
'Super Sioux' (Standard) Semideterminate		70 days	This tomato, developed by the Nebraska A.E.S., is a reliable producer of medium-size (6 oz.) smooth round fruits. The rather open vine is best grown in a wire cage. 'Super Sioux' is noteworthy for its ability to set fruit in high temperatures. Widely available.
'Bonny Best' (Standard) Indeterminate		70 days	Some experts think it is an obsolete variety, and others consider 'Bonny Best' an old-fashioned favorite. The smooth, meaty, small (4 oz.) fruits are borne in clusters. It's best to grow this tomato in a wire cage to avoid sunscald and to increase the yield. Widely available.
'Moreton Hybrid' (Hybrid) Indeterminate Verticillium wilt Fusarium wilt		70 days	A long-time favorite in the Northeast, developed by the Joseph Harris Seed Co. The fruits are medium-size (6 to 8 oz.), firm, and meaty. The vine is vigorous and produces a heavy foliage cover. 'Moreton Hybrid' can be grown in a cage or on stakes or trellises. Recommended by Agricultural Extension Services in Minnesota, Ohio, Delaware, Maine, New Hampshire, Rhode Island, and Vermont, and also reported successful in Louisiana and Oregon. Available: (13).

Shape, Name, and Disease Resistance	Region Best Adapted	Transplant to Harvest	Description
'Fantastic' (Hybrid) Indeterminate		70 days	'Fantastic' is a rugged hybrid with wide adaptation developed by the Petoseed Co. It produces a high yield of smooth, medium-large (8 oz.) fruit, similar to 'Moreton Hybrid' (see page 117). The plants continue bearing until frost. Widely available.
'Super Fantastic VF' (Hybrid) Indeterminate Verticillium wilt Fusarium wilt		70 days	'Super Fantastic VF' differs from 'Fantastic' in several ways. The shape of the fruit is deep oblate to round, and it has the added benefit of disease resistance. Like 'Fantastic' it produces heavy yields right up until frost. A George Ball introduction; widely available in nurseries as transplants. Available: (53).
'Terrific' (Hybrid) Indeterminate Verticillium wilt Fusarium wilt Nematodes		70 days	'Terrific' produces large (8 to 10 oz.) fruits over a long season. The tomatoes are smooth, firm, and meaty, and have good crack resistance. The vines are strong growing, with good foliage cover. This rugged hybrid should be grown in a cage or on a trellis. Widely available.
'Redpak' (Hybrid) Determinate Verticillium wilt Fusarium wilt		71 days	This relatively new variety, introduced by Harris Seed Co., bears large, unusually firm fruits with practically solid flesh. The tomatoes hold well on the vine and are resistant to cracking. When the plants are mature, the leaves of the small, compact vines tend to curl, but this has no effect on the yield or quality of the tomatoes. Available: (13).
'Better Boy' (Hybrid) Indeterminate Verticillium wilt Fusarium wilt Nematodes		72 days	'Better Boy' is widely adapted and widely recommended as a main crop variety. It produces a heavy crop of very large (12 to 16 oz.) fruit, just right for slicing. The vines are vigorous and sturdy, and should be grown in a cage or on a trellis or stake. Give this variety a continuous supply of water to avoid blossom-end rot. Widely available.
'Floramerica' (Hybrid) Determinate Verticillium wilt Fusarium wilt		72 days	A 1978 All America Award winner, 'Floramerica' has tolerance of, or resistance to, 17 diseases or genetic disorders. Developed by the University of Florida, 'Floramerica' is a widely adapted tomato especially developed for home gardeners. The fruit is very red, large, and sets readily. Widely available.
'The Juice' (Hybrid) Determinate Verticillium wilt Fusarium wilt		72 days	As the name implies, 'The Juice' is a tasty, juicy tomato, medium to large in size. The attractive vine with its dark green foliage produces an abundance of tomatoes. A good variety to train in wire cages or on short stakes. Originated by the George Ball Co. Widely available.

'Marglobe'   'Better Boy'   'Jet Star'

'Fantastic' is a consistent producer of uniform tomatoes borne in clusters.

Midseason Varieties (continued)

Shape, Name, and Disease Resistance	Region Best Adapted	Transplant to Harvest	Description
'Burpee's VF' (Hybrid) Indeterminate Verticillium wilt Fusarium wilt		72 days	One of the most widely adapted and widely recommended hybrids. The fruit is firm, meaty, and medium to large (8 oz.), resistant to catfacing and cracking. The strong, sturdy vines have a heavy foliage cover. This tomato is the main-season favorite of its developer, the Burpee Seed Co. 'Burpee's VF' can be grown in a cage or on a stake or trellis. Available: (5), (27), (50), (51).
'Jet Star' (Hybrid) Indeterminate Verticillium wilt Fusarium wilt		72 days	This variety, developed by the Harris Seed Co., is important in the second early season. The medium-large (8 oz.) fruits are firm and set well. The vine is compact, with good foliage cover. 'Jet Star' is resistant to cracking, and should be grown in a cage or on a stake or trellis. Recommended by Agricultural Extension Services in western Washington, Idaho, and Oregon. Available: (13).
'Glamour' (Standard) Indeterminate		74 days	One of the first crack-resistant varieties, 'Glamour' was originally developed by the Bird's-Eye Horticultural Research Lab., New York. The tomatoes are bright red, firm, solid, and of medium size (6 oz.). The vines produce fine foliage with fair cover. 'Glamour' should be grown in a cage to prevent sunscald. Widely available.
'Campbell 1327' (Standard) Determinate Verticillium wilt Fusarium wilt		75 days	Originated by the Campbell Soup Co., this variety produces a firm, smooth, medium-large (7 oz.) fruit that is resistant to cracking. 'Campbell 1327' is a heavy producer that sets reliably under adverse conditions. The vine has a heavy foliage cover. Widely available.
'Big Set' (Hybrid) Determinate Verticillium wilt Fusarium wilt Nematodes		75 days	'Big Set' produces smooth, firm, meaty fruit in the large (8 to 9 oz.) category. It sets well under both low and high temperatures. The tomatoes are resistant to cracking, catfacing, and blossom-end rot. The vine is vigorous and compact, and can be caged or allowed to sprawl on the ground. This rugged hybrid was originally developed by the Petoseed Co. Available: (12), (22).

'Big Girl'

'Big Boy'

Midseason Varieties (continued)

Shape, Name, and Disease Resistance	Region Best Adapted	Transplant to Harvest	Description
'Bonus' (Hybrid) Determinate Verticillium wilt Fusarium wilt Nematodes		75 days	The fruits of 'Bonus' are medium-large (8 oz.), smooth, firm, and resistant to cracking and catfacing. This variety appears to have some ability to set under relatively high temperatures. 'Bonus' was developed by the Petoseed Co., and can be grown in a cage or on a short trellis. Available: (15), (21), (28), (37).
'Heinz 1350' (Standard) Determinate Verticillium wilt Fusarium wilt		75 days	This tomato is widely recommended and widely available. It was originally developed by the H.J. Heinz Co. The uniform, medium-size fruits have good crack resistance, and the strong, compact, determinate vines can be close-planted. Recommended by the Agricultural Extension Services in Oregon and Colorado. Widely available.
'Jim Dandy' (Hybrid) Indeterminate		75 days	'Jim Dandy' produces large red solid fruit on vigorous vines which set continuously and hold their size all season. Good for slicing and canning. The plants should be grown in a cage or on a stake. Write to the original developer, Ferry-Morse Seed Co., for availability. Available: (55).
'Manapal' (Standard) Indeterminate Fusarium wilt		75 days	'Manapal' is rated as one of the best home garden varieties in the South, and has proven itself in trials in Colorado and Idaho. It was originated by the Florida A.E.S. especially for humid growing conditions. 'Manapal' is also a highly productive greenhouse tomato throughout the South and Southwest, and has resistance to many foliage diseases. Available: (28), (30), (37).
'Marglobe' (Standard) Determinate Fusarium wilt		75 days	One of the grand old names in tomatoes. The medium-size (6 oz.) fruit is smooth, firm, and thick-walled. The vine growth is uniform and vigorous, with a good heavy foliage cover. Widely available.
'Monte Carlo' (Hybrid) Indeterminate Verticillium wilt Fusarium wilt Nematodes		75 days	A widely adapted variety that produces large (9 oz.) smooth fruits over a long season. In addition to its triple disease resistance, 'Monte Carlo' is also resistant to cracking, catfacing, sunscald, and blossom-end rot. The tall-growing, strong vines provide a good foliage cover. Widely available.

Midseason Varieties (continued)

Shape, Name, and Disease Resistance	Region Best Adapted	Transplant to Harvest	Description
'Walter' (Standard) Determinate Fusarium wilt		75 days	'Walter' is a reliable home garden performer, but must be harvested ripe. It has resistance to leaf diseases, cracking, catfacing, and blossom-end rot. The fruits are firm and of medium size (7 oz.). The compact vines provide good foliage cover; grow them on stakes or let them sprawl on the ground. Recommended by Agricultural Extension Services in Georgia, Maryland, and Tennessee. Available: (2), (28), (37).
'Atkinson' (Standard) Indeterminate Fusarium wilt Nematodes		75–80 days	Originated by Auburn University, this variety produces firm and meaty medium-size (6 oz.) tomatoes. The plant is a strong grower with good foliage protection and moderate resistance to early blight and gray leaf spot. 'Atkinson' can be grown in a cage or on a stake or trellis. Available: (15), (22), (24).
'Burpee's Delicious' (Standard) Indeterminate		77 days	The fruit of 'Burpee's Delicious' has an almost solid interior with very small seed cavities. The plant is a medium-strong grower with good foliage protection. The tomatoes are extra large and have resistance to cracking. Available: (5), (51).
'Heinz 1370' (Standard) Determinate Fusarium wilt		77 days	This tomato is very similar to 'Heinz 1350' (see page 120), but it has less resistance and bears a few days later. It reputedly gives a high yield on second pickings. Recommended in Iowa, Illinois, Indiana, Ohio, and New Hampshire. Available: (27), (28), (32).
'Burpee's Big Boy' (Hybrid) Indeterminate		78 days	This name is probably the number one among tomatoes for the home garden. The very large (12 + oz.) fruits are firm, smooth, and thick-walled, and the vines produce continuously until frost. Widely available.
'Burpee's Big Girl' (Hybrid) Indeterminate Verticillium wilt Fusarium wilt		78 days	'Burpee's Big Girl' is a rugged hybrid of wide adaptation. It has all the good qualities of 'Big Boy' with the added advantage of disease resistance. Available: (5).
'Supersonic' (Hybrid) Semideterminate Verticillium wilt Fusarium wilt		79 days	A widely adapted and widely recommended variety that produces heavy yields of large-size (9 oz.), fleshy, firm tomatoes with crack resistance. This rugged hybrid developed by the Harris Seed Co. is a strong-growing leafy plant that should be grown in a wire cage or on a trellis. Recommended by Agricultural Extension Services in Illinois, Iowa, Michigan, Missouri, Ohio, Wisconsin, Connecticut, Delaware, New Hampshire, New York, and Pennsylvania. Available: (13).
'Marion' (Standard) Indeterminate Fusarium wilt		79 days	Originated by the Clemson A.E.S., this is one of the best home garden stake varieties in the South. The medium-size (6 oz.) firm fruit is resistant to cracking. The vine is strong and vigorous, with good foliage cover, and is resistant to leaf mold and gray leaf spot. This tomato can be grown in a cage or on a stake or trellis. Recommended by Agricultural Extension Services in Georgia, Minnesota, South Carolina, and Virginia. Available: (15), (21), (22), (28).

'Wonder Boy'

'Rutgers'

'Ramapo'

Late Season Varieties

Shape, Name, and Disease Resistance	Region Best Adapted	Transplant to Harvest	Description
'Ramapo' (Hybrid) Indeterminate Verticillium wilt Fusarium wilt		80 days	This release from Rutgers University sets well under adverse conditions. The fruit is deep crimson with thick walls, and of medium size (8 to 9 oz.), with resistance to cracking and blossom-end rot. The strong-growing, vigorous vine can be grown in a cage or on a stake or trellis. Available: (5), (13), (50).
'Rutgers Hybrid F' (Hybrid) Semideterminate Fusarium wilt		80 days	In 1964, Rutgers University introduced 'Rutgers Hybrid F'. It was a 'Rutgers' type of tomato with resistance to fusarium wilt. This introduction replaced the original 'Rutgers', and with all catalog listings, this is the variety you get. Widely available.
'Rutgers Hybrid VF' (Hybrid) Semideterminate Verticillium wilt Fusarium wilt		80 days	Since the introduction of this hybrid, several seed companies have introduced 'Rutgers' with both verticillium and fusarium resistance. These are 'Rutgers'-type tomatoes, but not the same as the original 'Rutgers'. Dr. Bernard Pollack, who introduced 'Rutgers Hybrid F', is the originator of 'Ramapo', which is a 'Rutgers' type with both fusarium and verticillium resistance. 'Rutgers VF' plants are available at many nurseries. Available: (13).
'Wonder Boy' (Hybrid) Indeterminate Verticillium wilt Fusarium wilt Nematodes		80 days	The well-known 'Wonder Boy VF' is being discontinued because of the addition of nematode resistance to this variety. It is a heavy producer of medium-large, firm fruits. The vine is strong, with medium foliage cover. Widely available.
'Vineripe' (Hybrid) Indeterminate Verticillium wilt Fusarium wilt Nematodes		80 days	'Vineripe' is one of the better quality hybrid tomatoes, with heavy yields of smooth, medium-firm, large (9 oz.) fruits. The vine is vigorous, with good leaf cover. Developed by Petoseed Co. Available: (21), (26).

Late Season Varieties (continued)

Shape, Name, and Disease Resistance	Region Best Adapted	Transplant to Harvest	Description
'Red Chief VFN' (Hybrid) Indeterminate Verticillium wilt Fusarium wilt Nematodes		80 days	A very red, deep globe-shaped tomato with excellent flavor. The vigorous vines bear over an extended season. Available: (15).
'He Man' (Hybrid) Strong indeterminate Verticillium wilt Fusarium wilt		82 days	A Goldsmith Seeds, Inc. introduction, with high yields of medium-firm, medium-size (6 oz.) uniform fruit. The vigorous vines should be staked or grown in a cage. Available: (18), (21), (29), (41).
'Homestead 24' (Standard) Determinate Fusarium wilt		82 days	'Homestead 24' is a consistent performer throughout the South. It sets fruit well under a wide variety of conditions, especially in high temperatures. The fruits are firm, smooth, and meaty, of medium size (8 oz.), and resistant to catfacing. The vines are medium-large, with a good foliage cover. This southern favorite, developed by the Asgrow Seed Co., is recommended by Agricultural Extension Services in Arkansas, Florida, Georgia, Oklahoma, and Virginia. Widely available.
'Brimmer' (Standard) Indeterminate		85 days	'Brimmer' tomatoes are large, well shaped, purplish pink, and frequently weigh over 1 pound. Although 'Brimmer' is a "Beefsteak" type, the fruit is meaty, with few seeds and no core. It is smoother and less likely to catface than other "Beefsteak" types. This is a good slicing tomato, grown best in a cage or on a stake. It is an old favorite in the Atlanta area. Available: (15), (22), (32).
'Indian River' (Standard) Indeterminate Fusarium wilt		85 days	Developed by the Florida A.E.S., this variety produces scarlet red, medium-size (6 oz.) fruit with thick walls and firm flesh. 'Indian River' tomatoes are noted for their small blossom-end scars. The vigorous vines yield well under warm, humid conditions and are resistant to leaf mold and gray leaf spot. Plants widely available in nurseries.
'Oxheart' (Standard) Indeterminate		86 days	This old-time tomato has unusual heart-shaped fruits that frequently weigh up to 2 pounds. The tomatoes are pink in color, with firm, meaty, solid flesh. The vines are large and open, requiring a cage to protect fruit from sunscald. Widely available.
'Manalucie' (Standard) Indeterminate Fusarium wilt		87 days	'Manalucie' is a southern favorite, with firm, meaty, thick-walled, medium-size (7 oz.) fruit. The tomatoes are resistant to cracking, sunscald, and blossom-end rot. The vines are upright and vigorous, with good leaf cover resistant to leaf mold and gray leaf spot. It is best grown in a cage or on a stake or trellis. Recommended by Agricultural Extension Services in Florida, Maryland, Mississippi, and South Carolina. Available: (5), (15), (21), (28), (49), (50).
'Bragger' (Hybrid) Indeterminate		87 days	'Bragger' produces large (13 oz. and larger) red, meaty tomatoes with resistance to cracking. The strong-growing vines have large leaves. The recommended practice is to prune the vines to one stem and grow them in a cage or on a stake. Available: (21), (41).

Beefsteak Varieties

"Beefsteak' is one of the magic words in almost any general discussion of tomato varieties. The word is used to describe a type rather than a specific variety—although there is a legitimate variety named 'Beefsteak'.

To most consumers "Beefsteak" means a large tomato in which the flesh is thick and solid with a few small seed cavities.

Where summers are short, the following varieties requiring a warm season of 80 to 90 days are a poor risk. Note the early "Beefsteaks."

A new late season variety. Burpee Seed Co. is testing a unique, long-keeping tomato, developed from seeds provided by an Ohio restaurateur who harvested fresh tomatoes for her customers *through the fall and winter*!

Beefsteak Varieties

Shape, Name, and Disease Resistance	Region Best Adapted	Transplant to Harvest	Description
'Bush Beefsteak' (Standard) Compact determinate		62 days	This variety sets a good crop of tomatoes under most adverse conditions. The fruit is large (8 oz.) and firm. Available: (27), (38), (40), (41), (42).
'Prime Beefsteak' (Hybrid) Determinate Verticillium wilt Fusarium wilt		70 days	This hybrid earns the name "Beefsteak" because of its meaty character. The fruit is large (8 to 10 oz.) and smoother than that of the regular 'Beefsteak'. This vigorous tomato was developed by the Ferry-Morse Seed Co. Available: (55).
'Olympic' (Standard) Indeterminate Fusarium wilt		76 days	'Olympic' produces medium to large pink tomatoes with good crack resistance. A popular tomato in the Montreal area. Available: (27).
'Beefmaster' (Hybrid) Indeterminate Verticillium wilt Fusarium wilt Nematodes		80 days	Formerly named 'Beefeater', this variety developed by the Petoseed Co. produces large fruit (to 2 lbs.) on a vigorous vine. Widely available.
'Burpee's Supersteak' (Hybrid) Indeterminate Verticillium wilt Fusarium wilt Nematodes		80 days	These tomatoes have consistent texture and size; they are particularly good for slicing. Available: (5).
'Pink Ponderosa' (Standard) Indeterminate		90 days	This is an old-time variety that produces large (to 2 lbs.) tomatoes that are meaty and firm. The vine is large and vigorous but provides little sunscald protection. To protect fruits it is best to grow it in a wire cage. 'Red Ponderosa' is similar, but deep scarlet in color. Widely available.
'Beefsteak' (Standard) Indeterminate		90 days	Originally called 'Crimson Cushion', this variety produces ribbed, irregular, rough fruit. The vine is vigorous, with rough foliage, and is best grown in a cage. Widely available.

The 'Long-Keeper' tomato stores for 6 to 12 weeks extremely well, though test results have not yet established the best harvesting and storing methods. Some fruits do best on open shelves in a moderately cool place; others, on a sunny windowsill. Its taste, though less distinguished than a midseason variety ripened on the vine, surpasses the "store-bought" varieties available in December or January.

Burpee trials suggest the 'Long-Keeper' does best when started 4 to 6 weeks after main-crop varieties are sown, and in wire cages or tomato towers to keep fruits clean and blemish-free.

'Yellow Plum'

'Large Red Cherry'

Small-Fruit Varieties

The small-fruited tomatoes should be considered as a special class. They are rank indeterminate growers capable of producing fruit under the most adverse conditions. They seem to be unaffected by diseases that cut short the life of the large-fruited varieties and set fruit where other varieties fail.

Actually, they are not disease-resistant or immune to blossom drop. The reason they succeed where others fail is the tremendous number of blossoms per plant. If you lose a few, you still have a good yield. The stamina of these small-fruited forms is particularly advantageous in areas too hot for normal tomato growing.

'Large Red Cherry' can be grown in a hanging basket indoors in a well-lighted window.

Small-Fruited Varieties

Shape, Name, and Disease Resistance	Region Best Adapted	Transplant to Harvest	Description
'Cherry Grande' (Hybrid) Determinate Verticillium wilt Fusarium wilt		58 days	This variety produces large, 1½-inch fruit, heavily set on a vigorous vine. Broad foliage provides good protection for these cherry tomatoes. Available: (28).
'Sweet 100' (Hybrid) Indeterminate		62 days	Very large multiple-branched clusters of 1-inch fruit abound on these plants. The vigorous vine benefits from pruning, caging, or staking. Sweet, flavorful, and high in vitamin C, they're great in salads. Available: (5), (18), (21), (28), (36), (41).
'Large Red Cherry' (Standard) Indeterminate		70 days	These redskinned cherry-type tomatoes grow to be 1½ inches round. Borne in clusters, the plants are highly productive. A nice addition to salads. Available: (12).
'Yellow Plum' (Hybrid) Indeterminate		70 days	These plum-shaped yellow tomatoes grow to be 1½ inches in diameter. The plants bear many-fruited clusters right up to frost. Ideal in preserves or salads. Available: (12), (18).
'Red Pear' (Standard) Indeterminate		70 days	Clusters of pear-shaped fruits are scarlet red, 1¾ to 2 inches long, and 1 inch in diameter. Tasty in salads. Available: (10), (12), (21).
'Yellow Pear' (Standard) Indeterminate		76 days	These old-fashioned, pear-shaped tomatoes grow to an average length of 1¾ to 2 inches long. Fruit is borne in clusters. Mild-flavored, they're best for preserving and pickling, but also can add unusual shape and color to salads. Available: (10), (12), (21).

'Yellow Pear'

'Sweet 100'

Container Varieties

Plant breeders have developed a number of cultivars that can be grouped as "container" tomatoes. Actually, any tomato can be grown in a container, but the following varieties are well-adapted to grow attractively in containers.

Container Varieties

Shape, Name, and Disease Resistance	Region Best Adapted	Transplant to Harvest	Description
'Burgess Early Salad' (Hybrid) Determinate		45 days	'Burgess Early Salad' is an unusual tomato that produces 250 to 300 1½-inch fruits on a vine only 6 to 8 inches tall. It's not unusual for the plant to spread 2 feet or more, making it a good candidate for container or hanging basket culture. Available: (21).
'Pixie Hybrid' (Hybrid) Determinate		52 days	This early-ripening tomato can be grown in pots or directly in the garden. The fruit is approximately 1¾ inches in diameter and is produced on a 14- to 18-inch plant. If you grow it in the garden, give it a short wire cage to prevent sunscald. This variety will also produce tomatoes indoors in winter, given a warm sunny location. Available: (1), (5).
'Tiny Tim' (Standard) Determinate		55 days	'Tiny Tim' produces the smallest-size fruit of the group: only ¾-inch in diameter. The scarlet red tomatoes are highly decorative and can be grown in a hanging basket with a 6-inch pot. Vines grow to about 15 inches. Widely available.
'Salad Top' (Standard) Determinate		60 days	A miniature compact vine, less than 8 inches tall, produces a good crop of 1-inch fruits. Can be planted in a 6-inch pot, or two plants to an 8-inch pot. Widely available in nurseries as transplants. Available: (53).
'Small Fry' (Hybrid) Determinate Verticillium wilt Fusarium wilt Nematodes		60 days	'Small Fry' produces cherry-type, 1-inch fruit in clusters on a 40-inch vine. This 1970 All America Selection winner is a very heavy cropper. It can be grown in a container and trained on a trellis, or grown in the vegetable garden using a small wire cage. Produces throughout the growing season. Widely available.
'Presto Hybrid' (Hybrid) Determinate		60 days	This variety is recommended as an early variety for the home garden. The small vine (less than 2 feet) has small leaves and produces a heavy load of tomatoes, each about the size of a half-dollar. 'Presto Hybrid' can be grown in a 10- or 12-inch pot or tub and trained on a stake or small trellis. Available: (13).

Container Varieties (continued)

Shape, Name, and Disease Resistance	Region Best Adapted	Transplant to Harvest	Description
'CB–City Best' (Hybrid) Determinate · Verticillium wilt · Fusarium wilt		60 days	Excellent flavor and heavy yields of medium-size fruit make this tomato a favorite. The foliage is lush and deep green and the branches self-supporting. An attractive container plant. Available: (21).
'Gardener's Delight' (Standard) Determinate		65 days	'Gardener's Delight' produces very sweet ¾-inch fruit in great abundance all summer. The tomatoes are crack-resistant and ripen well. Bright red, borne in clusters of 6 to 12 fruits, these small tomatoes are among the sweetest and best tasting. Available: (5).
'Toy Boy' (Hybrid) Determinate · Verticillium wilt · Fusarium wilt		68 days	Fruits the size of ping-pong balls are produced on a 12- to 14-inch plant. 'Toy Boy' can be grown three or four to a single 10-inch hanging basket or pot, outdoors or indoors with plenty of sunlight. Widely available as transplants at your nursery. Available: (56).
'Sugar Lump' (Standard) Determinate		70 days	This unusually sweet, cherry-size tomato is produced in clusters. The vine grows to about 30 inches and can be grown in a hanging basket or trained on a trellis. Available: (2), (16), (21), (36), (39).
'Patio Hybrid' (Hybrid) Determinate · Fusarium wilt		70 days	This variety produces a good yield of 2-inch fruits on a tree-like 24-inch plant which needs the support of a short stake when the fruit matures. It grows well in a 12-inch pot, but you can have an ornamental effect if you grow several together in a tub or 2-gallon box. Widely available.
'Tumblin' Tom' (Hybrid) Determinate		72 days	'Tumblin' Tom' provides an early and abundant yield of 1½- to 2-inch fruit on 20- to 24-inch vines. This variety can be grown in hanging baskets, 2-gallon containers, or window boxes. Widely available as transplants in nurseries. Available: (53).
'Stakeless' (Standard) Determinate · Fusarium wilt		78 days	'Stakeless' is an unusual plant, with dense foliage and leaves like those of a potato plant. Fruits are medium to large (6 to 8 oz.) and mild in flavor. The heavy stemmed, 18-inch vine needs no staking. We found it most interesting when grown in a box (12 inches wide and 8 inches deep) but gave it the support of short stakes when it became loaded with fruits. Given deep soil in the garden, 'Stakeless' grew 3 feet wide with a heavy yield of tomatoes. Available: (6), (27).

'Patio'

'Sugar Lump'

'Pixie'

'Tumblin Tom'

'Sunray'

Yellow-Orange Varieties

For years the yellow tomatoes have been praised for their "mild flavor and low acidity." Catalog writers and consumers erroneously concluded that mild flavor meant low acidity. Actually, the yellow tomatoes are just as acid as the red tomatoes. Today home canners are being warned even against mixing them with red tomatoes in any form of processing. This warning is unjustified. For more information about acidity see page 110.

White Varieties

Many white varieties are tall-growing, indeterminate vines that need training on a trellis or in a cage. The numbers following the varietal listing refer to the numbered list of seed companies on pages 139 and 140, from which these varieties may be ordered.

- ☐ *'Snowball'*. (78 days). Available: (10), (26), (38).
- ☐ *'White Beauty'*. (84 days). Available: (20), (21), (39).
- ☐ *'White Wonder'*. (85 days). Available: (16).

'Snowball'

'Golden Boy'

'Jubilee'

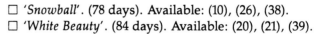
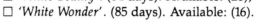

Yellow-Orange Varieties

Shape, Name, and Disease Resistance	Region Best Adapted	Transplant to Harvest	Description
'Golden Delight' (Standard) Determinate		65 days	Developed by South Dakota State University, 'Golden Delight' is the only early yellow variety. Available: (12), (33).
'Sunray' (Standard) Indeterminate Fusarium wilt		80 days	Originated by the U.S.D.A., 'Sunray' is similar to 'Jubilee' but with the addition of resistance to fusarium wilt. Widely available.
'Golden Boy' (Hybrid) Indeterminate		75–80 days	'Golden Boy' is the only hybrid in the yellow tomato group. It was originally developed by Petoseed Co. Widely available.
'Jubilee' (Standard) Indeterminate		80 days	This old-time variety was developed by the Burpee Seed Co. Widely available.
'Caro Red' (Standard)		80 days	'Caro Red' was developed by Purdue University. Its unique trait is that the tomatoes contain ten times the Provitamin A of standard tomatoes. Available: (9), (12), (16).

Paste Varieties

Home gardeners who make their own catsup, put up whole tomatoes, or can tomato paste manage to find room for a vine or two of the paste tomatoes. All bear generous crops of small, pear-shaped fruits on strong-growing vines.

'Chico III' 'Royal Chico' 'Roma' 'San Marzano'

Paste Varieties

Shape, Name, and Disease Resistance	Region Best Adapted	Transplant to Harvest	Description
'Napoli' (Standard) Medium determinate Verticillium wilt Fusarium wilt		63 days	This variety produces large yields of pear- to plum-shaped fruit, similar to 'Roma VF' but with a greater concentration at maturity. The vines provide good foliage cover. Available: (55).
'Nova' (Standard) Determinate Verticillium wilt Fusarium wilt		65 days	'Nova' is an early 'Roma'-type tomato developed by the New York A.E.S. It is the best choice for areas with short growing seasons. Available: (27).
'Veeroma' (Standard) Determinate Verticillium wilt Fusarium wilt		72 days	An improved 'Roma'-type tomato with less cracking. This smallish vine is a vigorous producer of excellent quality paste tomatoes. Available: (27).
'Roma' (Standard) Determinate Verticillium wilt Fusarium wilt		75 days	'Roma' is a widely recommended paste variety developed by Harris Seed Co. The vine is strong-growing, with heavy foliage cover. Widely available.
'Chico III' (Standard) Determinate Fusarium wilt		75 days	The fleshy fruits of 'Chico III' can be easily processed for juice. This variety will set fruit at high temperatures (76–77° at night and 96–97° F. during the day). The vines are compact and slightly open-growing. Available: (23), (50).
'Royal Chico' (Standard) Determinate Verticillium wilt Fusarium wilt		75 days	The growth habit of 'Royal Chico', a tomato originated by the Petoseed Co., is better behaved than that of 'Roma'. Available: (28).
'San Marzano' (Standard) Indeterminate		80 days	The fruit of 'San Marzano' is larger and more rectangular than that of other paste tomatoes. The flesh is also drier than most. Widely available.

Seed Company Specials

Shape, Name, and Disease Resistance	Region Best Adapted	Transplant to Harvest	Description
'Improved Wayahead' (Standard) Indeterminate		63 days	A Jung Seed Co. special. The fruits are smooth, solid, and of good size for an early tomato. The vine bears early and continues to bear through the season. Available: (16).
'Vigor Boy' (Hybrid) Determinate Verticillium wilt Fusarium wilt Nematodes		63 days	A Gurney Seed Co. special. This variety produces heavy yields of smooth, meaty, even-ripening tomatoes that weigh from 6 ounces to 1 pound. Available: (12).
'Hy-X' (Hybrid) Determinate		67 days	A Henry Field Seed Co. special, 'Hy-X' provides large yields of bright scarlet, medium-size (4 to 6 oz.) fruit on a short bushy vine. This variety does especially well in semi-arid climates. Available: (10).
'Whopper' (Hybrid) Indeterminate		75 days	A Park Seed Co. special, 'Whopper' produces heavy yields of smooth, meaty, even-ripening fruits. The vine is vigorous and tall-growing, with good foliage cover. The fruit has good resistance to cracking and blossom-end rot. Widely adapted. Available: (21).
'Abraham Lincoln' (Hybrid) Indeterminate		78 days	An R.H. Shumway Seed Co. special, this old-time tomato was originally developed by Buckbee's Rockford Seed Farms in Illinois. The fruit is very large (1 to 2 lbs.), solid, firm, meaty, and remarkably free from cracks and seams. As many as nine tomatoes may grow in a cluster. The vine is sturdy and continues bearing until frost. Available: (26).
'Red Chief' (Hybrid) Indeterminate Verticillium wilt Fusarium wilt Nematodes		80 days	This hybrid has excellent wilt and nematode resistance. The fruit is large (9 oz.) and very smooth. The vines, vigorous and productive over a long season, can be grown in a cage or on a stake or trellis. Available: (15).

Western and Southwestern Regional and State Specials

Washington. The tomato climates in the state vary among: the cool Puget Sound areas; the warmer areas from Chehalis to Vancouver; and the warmer areas of Eastern Washington with a much higher percentage of possible sunshine.

Based on yearly trials at Mt. Vernon, Washington, the early-maturing varieties are the best bets: 'Pixie', 'Small Fry', 'Patio', 'Tiny Tim' (see list of container varieties), and 'Early Girl', 'Ultra Girl', 'New Yorker', and 'Jetfire'.

Trials reveal an interesting picture of the tomato's climatic adaptability. In the long cool summers of the Puget Sound area, no variety responds exactly as advertised. An early variety such as 'Early Girl', normally requiring about 45 days between transplanting time and first ripe fruit, requires 98 days at Mt. Vernon. At left is a comparison of the ideal growing season compared to actual time required in the Mt. Vernon trials.

Based on these trials and experience south of the Puget Sound area, Washington State University Experiment Stations in Puyallup and Vancouver recommend these varieties in addition: 'Springset', 'Jet Star', 'Fantastic', and 'IPB'.

The Washington Extension Service is making seeds available of a variety called 'IPB (Early Swedish)'. This tomato produces fruit that is medium to

	Number of days from setting out transplants to first ripe fruit	
Variety	Ideal	Mt. Vernon
'Early Girl'	(45 days)	98 days
'Jetfire'	(60 days)	119 days
'New Yorker'	(64 days)	112 days
'Springset'	(65 days)	112 days
'Fantastic'	(70 days)	119 days
'Jet Star'	(72 days)	119 days

small and crack-resistant. The vine is determinate, 3 to 4 feet tall, and the skin is tough. Its great virtue is that it will produce red-ripe tomatoes every year. If seed is not available locally, write to: 4-H Foundation, Cooperative Extension Service, 5601 6th Ave., Tacoma, WA 94806. This tomato was introduced years ago by Oregon State University under its full name, 'Immuna Prior Beta'.

Eastern Washington. The varieties recommended by the Agricultural Extension Service are: (Early season) 'Pixie', 'New Yorker'; (Midseason) 'Ace'.

Intermountain areas. The U.S.D.A. at the Prosser, Washington, Research Station has released four tomatoes bred for resistance to curly-top disease in western areas where this is a problem.

'Roza VF' sets heavily under adverse cold or hot conditions; fruits ripen over a short time and produce juice of good consistency. 'Columbia VF' has larger, later-maturing fruit, and has less curly-top resistance than 'Roza'.

'Rowpac' has the same disease resistance as 'Roza', but with smaller fruit, matures about a week earlier, makes good purée and juice, and is a good canner. 'Saladmaster VF' is an early, large cherry.

For information about obtaining seed, contact the Washington State Crop Improvement Association, Inc., 513 N. Front St., Yakima, WA 98901.

Western and Southwestern Regional Specials

Shape, Name, and Disease Resistance	Region Best Adapted	Transplant to Harvest	Description
'Pakmore' (Standard) Medium determinate / Verticillium wilt / Fusarium wilt	NV, UT, CO, CA, AZ, NM	75 days	A 'Pearson' type of tomato developed by the University of California, 'Pakmore' provides a big harvest of large tomatoes. It is best grown in a large cage. Recommended by Agricultural Extension Services in Arizona, California, and Colorado. Plants widely available at nurseries.
'VFN 8' (Standard) Medium determinate / Verticillium wilt / Fusarium wilt / Nematodes	CA	75 days	'VFN 8' was developed by the University of California and produces medium to large fruits that hold up well after fall rains. Widely available in California.
'Ace-Hy' (Hybrid) Determinate / Verticillium wilt / Fusarium wilt / Nematodes	CA	76 days	The fruits of this tomato are smooth, and the roots are resistant to root-knot nematode—a special consideration for many areas of California. Widely available in California.
'Ace 55' (Standard) Medium determinate / Verticillium wilt / Fusarium wilt	WA, OR, ID, NV, UT, CA, AZ	76 days	Although the fruits of 'Ace 55' are not as smooth as the original 'Ace', the tomatoes are nonetheless 'Ace'-type, with disease resistance. Available: (2), (5), (49).
'VFN Bush' (Standard) Determinate / Verticillium wilt / Fusarium wilt / Nematodes	CA	80 days	The fruit of this variety is medium-size (6 oz.), firm, and smooth. The vine is compact with good foliage cover. Developed by the Petoseed Co. Widely available.
'Cal-Ace' (Standard) Semideterminate / Verticillium wilt / Fusarium wilt	WA, OR, ID, NV, UT, CA, AZ	80 days	This variety has smoother fruit and a heavier fruit set than the original 'Ace', with the added benefit of disease resistance. Available: (6), (28), (50).

Shape, Name, and Disease Resistance	Region Best Adapted	Transplant to Harvest	Description
'Hybrid Ace' (Hybrid) Determinate Verticillium wilt Fusarium wilt Nematodes		80 days	This is an 'Ace'-type with resistance to nematodes and wilt diseases, developed by the Petoseed Co. All of the 'Ace' varieties are strong growing, and need the support of a stake, trellis, or cage. They are well adapted to the hot, dry summer areas of the West where a medium-late tomato will ripen. Available: (53).
'Royal Ace' (Standard) Determinate Verticillium wilt Fusarium wilt		80 days	Originated by the Ferry-Morse Seed Co., this tomato is similar to 'Ace' but tends to hold its size better and averages larger fruits than the original variety. Available: (55).
'Early Pak 7' (Standard) Large determinate		82 days	Originated by the Ferry Morse Seed Co., 'Early Pak 7' produces medium-firm, medium-large (8 oz.) fruits on a large but compact vine. Foliage provides fair cover, but for best sunscald protection the plant should be grown in a cage or on a trellis. Plants widely available at nurseries. Available: (55).
'Early Pak 707' (Standard) Large determinate Verticillium wilt Fusarium wilt		82 days	This variety is more uniform, smoother, and more disease resistant than 'Early Pak 7'. Plants widely available at nurseries. Available: (55).
'Pearson A-1 Improved' (Standard) Medium determinate		90 days	An old-time favorite in the West, 'Pearson A-1 Improved' is a Ferry-Morse Seed Co. selection with smoother but slightly smaller fruits (7 oz.) than the original 'Pearson A-1'. Widely available.
'Pearson Improved' (Standard) Medium determinate Verticillium wilt Fusarium wilt		90 days	Developed by the Petoseed Co., 'Pearson Improved' produces large (8 oz.) tomatoes on a somewhat open vine. The plant has concentrated disease resistance and is best grown in a cage. Available: (56).

Oregon. Western Oregon offers a progressively warmer climate from Portland south to Medford. The Oregon Agricultural Extension Service's recommended list includes: (Early season) 'New Yorker', 'Early Girl'; (Mid-season) 'Big Early Hybrid', 'Springset', 'Spring Giant', 'Early Pak 707', 'Heinz 1350', 'Willamette', 'Redpak'; (Late season) 'Ace', 'Big Boy', 'Morton Hybrid', 'Jet Star'.

Of the varieties mentioned above, 'Willamette' is a time-tested and consistent top performer in central-western Oregon.

Oregon Specials

Shape, Name, and Disease Resistance	Region Best Adapted	Transplant to Harvest	Description
'Willamette' (Standard) Determinate		67 days	This variety is always in the top five in Oregon trials. It was developed by the Oregon A.E.S. and produces medium-size, round, firm fruits with some crack resistance. The size of the tomatoes decreases as the season progresses. The vine is medium large. Available in local seed racks.

Arizona. The varieties adapted to California interior areas are generally recommended for Arizona: 'Early Pak 7', 'Early Pak 707', 'Ace 55', 'Cal-Ace', 'Pearson Improved', 'Pakmore', and 'VFN 8'.

Texas specials. Although Texas is not classed as a western state, it has developed varieties well suited to all areas that have hot, dry summers.

To be a success in Texas, a tomato should be able to set fruit in high temperatures—90°F. days and 78°F. nights. Heat resistance is an important factor in the tomato breeding program at Texas A&M University.

Are there varieties that adapt to all climates—from humid to arid? Sam Cotner, Vegetable Specialist at Texas A&M, Agricultural Extension Service, answered the question this way: "If forced to name varieties suited to the many climates of the state, I would first divide the state east and west by drawing a line from Dallas through Waco; East Texas would be east of the line."

Sam Cotner's choices of cultivars for these two regions are the following:

East Texas

'Better Boy'	'Homestead 24'	'Springset'
'Big Set'	'Porter'	'Supermarket'
'Chico III'	'Saladette'	'Terrific'
'Gulf States Market'	'Spring Giant'	'Walter'

West Texas

'Big Set'	'Saladette'
'Bonus'	'Spring Giant'
'Chico III'	'Walter'

Particulars on all varieties listed are given throughout this chapter. Following are brief descriptions of some of the Texas specials.

Texas Specials

Shape, Name, and Disease Resistance	Region Best Adapted	Transplant to Harvest	Description
'Improved Porter' (Standard) (Porter's Pride) Indeterminate		65 days	This improved tomato bears firm, uniform, medium-size fruits that have a meaty texture and scarlet red color. The vine is vigorous and has good foliage protection. 'Improved Porter' provides heavy crops right up until frost. Available: (30), (37).
'Porter' (Standard) Indeterminate		65 days	This old-time favorite was developed by the Porter Seed Co. It produces tomatoes about the size of a pullet egg, of good quality and flavor. The fruits have pinkish skin, and the vine is relatively large, with good foliage cover. Porter's catalog describes it as the "old reliable." It produces consistently over a wide range of climatic and soil conditions. Because of its heat resistance, 'Porter' can be started later than other varieties and still produce good summer and fall crops. Available: (30), (37).
'Plainsman' (Standard) Determinate		65 days	Originated at the Texas A.E.S., 'Plainsman' produces medium-size (5 oz.) smooth fruits that are borne together in clusters. The plants are very compact and can be planted close together or in small wire cages. Available: (6), (37).

Texas Specials (continued)

Shape, Name, and Disease Resistance	Region Best Adapted	Transplant to Harvest	Description
'Saladette' (Standard) Determinate Fusarium wilt		65 days	These flavorful tomatoes are about the size and shape of a large plum (average 2 oz.). The fruit is thick-walled, meaty, firm, and crack-resistant. The vines are small and compact, with a 14- to 16-inch spread. 'Saladette' will produce heavy crops under adverse conditions of high heat and humidity. Available: (30), (37), (41).
'Hotset' (Standard) Indeterminate		72 days	These smooth, medium-large (8 oz.) tomatoes have resistance to sunscald, puffiness, and catfacing. The catalog description says: " 'Hotset' bears tomatoes when summer temperatures cause blossom sterility in many other varieties." It continues to set fruit when day temperatures are as high as 90° F. The vine is large and productive. Available: (37).
'Young' (Standard) Semideterminate Fusarium wilt		72 days	These tomatoes have good resistance to cracking, blossom-end rot, catfacing, and puffing. The fruit is firm, dark red, medium to large (8 to 9 oz.), and the vines bear good yields. Available: (37).
'Nematex' (Standard) Determinate Fusarium wilt Nematodes		75 days	A heavy producer of medium-size (6 to 8 oz.) round, smooth, solid tomatoes. The bush-type vine has sufficient foliage cover for good fruit protection. This variety is resistant to most types of nematodes. Available: (37).

Midwest/North Regional Specials

Shape, Name, and Disease Resistance	Region Best Adapted	Transplant to Harvest	Description
'Lark' (Standard) Determinate	ND	59 days	'Lark' is a very early producer of firm tomatoes. The plant is compact and the fruits are resistant to cracking and catfacing. Available locally.
'Sun Up' (Hybrid) Determinate Fusarium wilt	MO	60 days	This is a compact bush form of the 'Fireball' type (see page 116), but with larger fruit and better foliage cover. Fruit set is concentrated in a short period. Available: (18), (51).

Shape, Name, and Disease Resistance	Region Best Adapted	Transplant to Harvest	Description
'Rushmore' (Hybrid) Semideterminate Verticillium wilt Fusarium wilt	SD	67 days	This variety was developed to withstand the cool springs and hot summers of the Midwest. 'Rushmore' produces heavy yields of medium-size, firm, meaty tomatoes. Available: (12), (18), (27).
'Mocross Surprise' (Hybrid) Strong indeterminate Fusarium wilt	MO	68 days	This tomato bears medium to large fruit that is smooth and firm. The plant is a heavy producer. For better flavor and color, allow the tomatoes to become fully ripe before picking. Available: (10), (11), (18), (41), (51).
'Tomboy' (Standard) Indeterminate	MO	68 days	This variety produces tomatoes similar to a "Beefsteak" variety. The fruits are large and meaty. The early-maturing tomatoes are rough, but tend to smooth out as the season advances, and they have some crack resistance. Available: (18), (51).
'Avalanche' (Hybrid) Indeterminate Fusarium wilt	MO	70 days	'Avalanche' has been a top yielder in Missouri trials for 5 years in a row. It sets fruit despite heat and drought conditions and produces medium-large tomatoes which are crack resistant. Can be grown in a cage or on a stake or trellis, or allowed to sprawl on the ground. Available: (11), (18), (51).
'Mocross Supreme' (Hybrid) Semideterminate Fusarium wilt	MO	70 days	For the old-timer who wants a tomato with green shoulders, this is the variety to pick. The medium-to-large fruit is smooth and firm. The plant produces a good, season-long crop, with some crack and wilt resistance. Available: (51).
'Cannonball' (Standard) Determinate	ND	71 days	A 'Spring Giant' type of tomato bred for North Dakota conditions. The fruit is firm and of medium size (6 to 7 oz.). Vines provide medium to heavy foliage cover. Available locally.
'Pink Gourmet' (Hybrid) Indeterminate Fusarium wilt	MO	72 days	An unusually early pink "Beefsteak"-type tomato. The fruit is firm and meaty. Available: (18), (51).
'Pink Delight' (Hybrid) Indeterminate Fusarium wilt	MO	72 days	This hybrid was released as a market type because of its resistance to cracking, and has now found acceptance in the home garden market. The fruit is very smooth and pink in color. The 'Arkansas Traveler' is one parent. Available: (18), (28), (51).
'Pink Savor' (Standard) Indeterminate	MO	75 days	'Pink Savor' is a pink plum-type tomato about twice the size of a large cherry tomato: an excellent "bite-size" tomato. Available locally.
'Redheart' (Hybrid) Indeterminate Fusarium wilt	MO	75 days	This tomato is a large 'Big Boy'-type. The fruit is large (up to 1 lb.), rough, and the flesh is solid. The vigorous vines are very productive. Available locally.

Southern Regional Specials

Shape, Name, and Disease Resistance	Region Best Adapted	Transplant to Harvest	Description
'Pelican' (Standard) Fusarium wilt Nematodes	LA	70 days	Originated by Louisiana State University, this variety is a good choice for home gardeners with a nematode problem. The fruit is red, smooth, slightly larger (8 oz.) than 'Creole' and ripens a few days earlier. 'Pelican' sets fruits under higher temperatures than most other tomatoes and offers good resistance to foliage diseases. Grow this variety in a cage or on a stake. Available: (22).
'Creole' (Standard) Indeterminate Fusarium wilt	LA	72 days	Another introduction from Louisiana State University, 'Creole' produces smooth, medium-size fruit with firm flesh of good texture. The plant sets fruit in high temperatures and bears an abundance of tomatoes. It is resistant to foliage diseases and blossom-end rot, and should be grown in a cage or on a stake. Available: (22).
'Floralou' (Hybrid) Indeterminate Fusarium wilt	LA	74 days	Although its fruits are smaller, this tomato will out-yield 'Floradel' (see page 137) on the fertile soils in Louisiana. 'Floralou' produces large yields of medium (5 oz.) fruits that are unusually uniform and deep red in color, with small seed cavities. The vine is very large, with a dense foliage cover resistant to several foliage diseases. Fruits are resistant to cracking and blossom-end rot. This variety should be grown in a cage or on a stake or trellis.
'Traveler' (Standard) Indeterminate Fusarium wilt	AK, MI, LA	78 days	This pink tomato has replaced both 'Bradley' and 'Gulf State Market' in commercial plantings in Louisiana. The fruits are of medium size (5 oz.) with good crack resistance. The vines produce good foliage cover. An improved selection released by the University of Arkansas is called 'Traveler 76'. Available: (37).
'Gulf State Market' (Standard) Indeterminate	TX	75 days	An old-time variety with pink skin and a solid, meaty texture. The tomatoes are small to medium (4 oz.) and resistant to cracking. The strong-growing vines with their good foliage cover bear over a long season. Available: (11), (22).
'Supermarket' (Standard) Determinate Fusarium wilt	TX	75 days	The Asgrow Seed Co. developed this smooth, firm, medium-size (5 to 6 oz.) tomato. The fruits have a very small blossom scar, are resistant to cracking and are very uniform in color. The medium-size vine has fair foliage cover and very good foliage disease resistance and should be grown in a short cage. Available as transplants at local nurseries.

Greenhouse Varieties

Shape, Name, and Disease Resistance	Region Best Adapted	Transplant to Harvest	Description
'Vendor' (Standard) Indeterminate	(U.S.)	63–65 days	Originated by Vineland Horticultural Research Institute, Ontario, Canada, 'Vendor' produces heavy yields of bright red, very firm, medium-size (6 to 8 oz.) fruit on a sturdy plant. The fruit ripens uniformly. The plants are shorter than most greenhouse types, and the fruit clusters are closer together than most varieties, making it easy to prune and pollinate. The small immature fruits sometimes appear egg-shaped, but fill out to a deep globe. The plants have resistance to leaf mold; the fruits resist cracking. Highly recommended for home garden growing. Available: (27), (36), (37), (40).

Greenhouse Varieties (continued)

Shape, Name, and Disease Resistance	Region Best Adapted	Transplant to Harvest	Description
'Michigan-Ohio' (Hybrid) Indeterminate Fusarium wilt		70–75 days	This hybrid, originated by the Michigan A.E.S., is known as "the most widely used and successful large red tomato for growing under glass or in plastic houses," and was especially developed for low-light greenhouse conditions. High yields of medium-large (8 oz.) fruit with thick walls come from the strong-growing, dark green, vigorous vines. Its chief limitation is lack of resistance to leaf mold, and in some areas it tends to blotch. Widely available.
'Ohio-Indiana' (Hybrid) Indeterminate Fusarium wilt		74 days	A medium-size pink tomato developed by the Ohio A.E.S., with a vine that is very productive and resistant to leaf mold. Customers in southern Ohio accept a red tomato, while those in the northern part of the state prefer a pink variety such as 'Ohio-Indiana'. Available: (21), (36), (40).
'Tuckcross 533' (Hybrid) Indeterminate Fusarium wilt		72–82 days	A tomato similar to 'Tuckcross 520', originated by the Missouri A.E.S. This variety tends to set fewer fruits, but of larger size. Additionally, it has resistance to leaf mold. Available: (27), (37), (40), (49).
'Tuckcross 520' (Hybrid) Indeterminate Fusarium wilt		74–82 days	One of the latest of the 'Tuckcross' series originated by the Missouri A.E.S. In addition to resistance to fusarium wilt, it has greatly improved resistance to races of leaf mold, has larger red fruit (6 to 8 oz.) and does not show the tendency to "over-flower" and "over-set" typical of the older 'Tuckcross' hybrids. Used as both a fall and spring crop, this variety will set fruit under adverse conditions. Available: (21), (28), (37), (40).
'Floradel' (Standard) Indeterminate Fusarium wilt		78 days	Originated by the Florida A.E.S. The medium-size (6 oz.) thick-walled fruit is produced on a large plant with heavy leaf cover. This tomato has resistance to fusarium wilt, gray leaf spot, and leaf mold. It grows best in a cage, on a trellis or staked. Available: (22), (28), (30), (37).

'Vendor'   'Tropic'

Greenhouse Varieties (continued)

Shape, Name, and Disease Resistance	Region Best Adapted	Transplant to Harvest	Description
'Tropic' (Standard) Indeterminate Verticillium wilt Fusarium wilt Nematodes		81 days	Developed by the University of Florida, this is a very strong newcomer and is one of the most popular greenhouse varieties. It produces good yields of very firm, large (8 to 9 oz.) fruit on a vigorous, strong-growing vine with good foliage cover; and it sets large fruit high on the vine to the end of the growing season. Multiple resistance to foliage diseases includes: gray leaf spot, graywall, leaf mold, early blight, and tolerance to races of tobacco mosaic. Also resistant to blossom-end rot. This tomato grows best in a cage or on a stake or trellis. Highly recommended for home garden growing as well as greenhouse culture. Available: (2), (5), (27), (28), (37).
'Manapal' (Standard) Indeterminate Fusarium wilt		81 days	This very widely adapted tomato developed by the Florida A.E.S. has smooth, firm, medium-size (6 oz.) thick-walled fruit on a large plant with heavy foliage cover. 'Manapal' has resistance to fusarium wilt, gray leaf spot and leaf mold, and is good for growing outdoors as well. Available: (28), (30), (37).

List of Catalog Sources

Throughout this chapter catalog sources of varieties that may be hard to find were given by a code number in parentheses. These numbers correspond to the numbers in the following listing, showing you which seed companies to write for the catalog you want.

In the listing of available catalogs there is a short description of each, with the total number of pages and the number of pages devoted to vegetables. Companies that are only vegetable specialists or cover the entire spectrum of garden plants can be determined by reading these descriptions.

Many of these seed catalogs are the equivalent of garden books and contain valuable reference material. They reward the careful reader.

Catalog entries change from year to year. What is scarce today may be widely available in future years, and vice versa, but a search uncovered the most likely sources of hard-to-find varieties.

Seed companies

Allen, Sterling & Lathrop (1)
191 U.S. Rt. #1
Falmouth, ME 04105
Straightforward listing of varieties and price. No descriptions.

Rocky Mountain Seed Co. (2)
1321–27 15th St.
Denver, CO 80217
64-page general catalog; vegetables, 20 pages. Features herbs, ornamental grasses, wild flowers.

Meyer Seed Co. (3)
600 So. Carolina St.
Baltimore, MD 21231
Vegetables, 23 pages. Features All-America Selections

Burgess Seed & Plant Co. (4)
P.O. Box 82
Galesburg, MI 49053
44 pages, 8½ × 11. Vegetables, 26 pages. Special attention to varieties for northern states. Many unusual items.

W. Atlee Burpee Co. (5)
Free from your nearest Burpee branch:
Warminster, PA 18974; Clinton, IA 52732;
Riverside, CA 92502
170 pages, 6 × 9. When seed catalogs are mentioned most people think "Burpee."

D. V. Burrell Seed Growers Co. (6)
Box 150
Rocky Ford, CO 81067
96 pages, 8½ × 4¼. Seed growers. Special emphasis on melons, peppers, tomatoes, and varieties for California and the Southwest.

Comstock, Ferre & Co. (7)
Wethersfield, CT 06109
20 pages, 8½ × 11. Vegetables, 11 pages. An informative guide to variety selection. 40 varieties of herbs. Founded 1820.

Jackson & Perkins (8)
Medford, OR 97501
The well-known name in roses adds the Jackson & Perkins Seedbook to their catalog list. 12 big pages on vegetables in the 40-page catalog.

Farmer Seed & Nursery Co. (9)
Faribault, MN 55021
84 pages, 8 × 10. Complete. Special attention to midget vegetables and early-maturing varieties for northern tier of states. Established 1888.

Henry Field Seed and Nursery Co. (10)
407 Sycamore St.
Shenandoah, IA 51601
116 pages, 8½ × 11. A complete catalogue. Wide variety selection. Many hard-to-find items, good tips for vegetable gardeners.

DeGiorgi Co., Inc. (11)
Council Bluffs, IA 51501
112 pages, 8½ × 11. Attention to the unusual. Established 1905. 35¢.

Gurney Seed & Nursery Co. (12)
1448 Page St.
Yankton, SD 57078
76 pages, 15 × 20. Emphasis on short-season North-country varieties. Accent on the unusual items.

Joseph Harris Co. (13)
Moreton Farm
Rochester, NY 14624
92 pages, 8½ × 11. Vegetables, 39 pages. The look of authority, and so considered, especially in the Northeast.

Charles C. Hart Seed Co. (14)
Box 169
Wethersfield, CT 06109
Vegetables, herbs, and flowers. 24 pages, including All-America Selections.

H. G. Hastings Co. (15)
P.O. Box 4274
Atlanta, GA 30302
64 pages, 8½ × 11. "85 years of service to the South." Complete southern garden guide.

J. W. Jung Seed Co. (16)
Station 8
Randolph, WI 53956
60 pages 9 × 12. Everything for the garden. Vegetables, 18 pages. Attention to Experiment Station introductions.

Earl May Seed & Nursery Co. (18)
Shenandoah, IA 51603
Complete catalog. 80 pages, 9½ × 12½. Wide choice of varities. Features All-America Selections.

Nichols Garden Nursery (19)
1190 No. Pacific Highway
Albany, OR 97321
88 pages, 8½ × 11. Written by an enthusiastic gardener and cook who has searched the world for the unusual and rare in vegetables and herbs.

L. L. Olds Seed Co. (20)
2901 Packers Ave., Box 1069
Madison, WI 53701
80 pages 8 × 10. Carefully written guide to varieties. All-America Selections; vegetables, 30 pages.

George W. Park Seed Co., Inc. (21)
Greenwood, SC 29646
122 pages, 8¼ × 11¼. A guide to quality and variety in flowers and vegetables. Includes indoor gardening. The most frequently "borrowed" seed catalog.

Reuter Seed Co., Inc. (22)
New Orleans, LA 70119
32 pages, 8 × 10. Vegetables, 16 pages. "Serving the South since 1881."

Seedway (23)
Hall, NY 14463
36 pages, 8½ × 11. Vegetables, 19 pages. Informative, straightforward presentation.

Roswell Seed Co. (24)
Box 725
Roswell, NM 88201
28 pages, 6 × 9. Vegetables, 12 pages. Special attention to varieties suited to the Southwest. Established 1900.

J. L. Hudson (25)
P.O. Box 1058
Redwood City, CA 94604
112 pages, 5½ × 9. Vegetables, 16 pages. Ask for vegetable catalog—it's free. General catalog, 50¢. Accent on the unusual. Wide selection of herbs.

R. H. Shumway, Seedsman (26)
628 Cedar St.
Rockford, IL 61101
88 pages, 10 × 13. Complete. Founded 1870. Catalog has maintained some of the "good farming" 1870 look.

Stokes Seeds (27)
Box 548 Main Post Office
Buffalo, NY 14240 and
St. Catherine's
Ontario, Canada
158 pages, 500 different vegetable and 800 different flower varieties. Emphasis on short-season strains. Canadian and European introductions.

Otis S. Twilley Seed Co. (28)
Salisbury, MD 21801
64 pages, 8½ × 11. Clear, helpful presentation with special attention to Experiment Station releases, and disease-resistant varieties, for varying climatic conditions.

Nicholson-Hardle Vegetable and Flower Seeds (30)
5717 West
Lovers TX 75209
15-page catalog stressing southern favorites.

Glecklers Seedmen (31)
Metamora, OH 43540
4 pages, 8½ × 14. Listings, brief descriptions of unusual, strange vegetables. Yearly supplements.

George Tait & Sons, Inc. (32)
900 Tidewater Dr.
Norfolk, VA 23504
Vegetables, 24 of 58 pages. Special varieties and planting information for eastern Virginia and North Carolina.

Vesey's Seeds, Ltd. (33)
York
Prince Edward Island, Canada
Features early vegetable varieties. Local planting information.

C. A. Cruickshank, Ltd. (34)
1015 Mount Pleasant Rd.
Toronto 12, Canada
An 80-page "garden guild" general catalog.

W. H. Perron & Co., Ltd. (36)
515 Labelle Blvd.
Laval, Quebec, Canada.
Complete general catalog of 106 pages.

Porter & Son, Seedsman (37)
Stephenville, TX 76401
30 pages, 12 pages on vegetables with emphasis on Texas varieties.

T & T Seeds, Ltd. (38)
120 Lombard Ave.
Winnipeg, Manitoba R3B OW3, Canada
48 pages, 6 × 8. Condensed general catalog for Midwest /North region. 25¢.

Dominion Seed House (39)
Georgetown, Ontario L7G 4A2, Canada
80 pages on vegetables in 180-page general catalog. Service (and catalog) exclusively for Canadian trade—no export.

Laval Seeds, Inc. (40)
3505 Boul. St.-Martin
Villa De Laval, Quebec, Canada
152-page general catalog. 57 pages on vegetables. (Printed in French only.)

A. E. McKenzie Co., Ltd., Seedsmen (41)
P.O. Box 1060
Brandon, Manitoba R7A 6E1, Canada

Alberta Nurseries and Seeds, Ltd. (42)
Box 29
Bowden, Alberta TOM OKO, Canada
48 pages, 7 × 10. Vegetables, 14 pages. Special attention to hardiness—short season.

Agway, Inc. (43)
Box 1333
Syracuse, NY 13201
56 pages, 8½ × 11. Thoughtfully prepared for northeastern states for their 700 retail outlets.

Johnny's Selected Seeds (44)
Albion, ME 04910
28 pages, 5½ × 8½. Heirloom beans and corn; many hard-to-find seeds of Oriental vegetables.

Kitazawa Seed Co. (45)
356 W. Taylor St.
San Jose, CA 95110
One-sheet listing of Oriental vegetables including bitter melon, Japanese pickling melon, gobo, and many varieties of more common Oriental vegetables.

J. A. Demonchaux Co. (46)
225 Jackson
Topeka, KS 66603
Gourmet garden seeds from France. 4-page list of vegetables and herbs.

Grace's Gardens (47)
100 Autumn Lane
Hackettstown, NJ 07840
16-page catalog of unusual seeds, "grow a complete 'believe it or not' food garden in less than ¼ acre." 25¢.

Tsang & Ma International (48)
1556 Laurel St.
San Carlos, CA 94070
1-page leaflet, 16 types of Chinese vegetables, including bitter melon and Chinese okra. $2 minimum order.

Burnett Brothers, Inc. (49)
92 Chambers St.
New York, NY 10007
48-page general catalog. Flower and vegetable seeds; garden supplies.

Archias Seed Store Corp. (51)
Box 109
Sedalia, MO 65301
42-page catalog includes vegetables, flowers, garden aids, roses, fruits, and berries. 13 pages of vegetable seeds.

Horticultural Enterprises (52)
Box 34082
Dallas, TX 75234
22-page catalog, 5½ × 8½. Entirely devoted to varieties of peppers and tomatillo.

Originators of varieties

Throughout the description of cultivars, the names of the originators of the cultivar are given. If the tomato cannot be located in the normal trade channels—seed racks, nursery transplants, or seed catalogs—it is suggested that the wholesale firm listed as the originator be contacted. This should be of help in finding a source.

George J. Ball, Inc. (53)
Box 355
West Chicago, IL 60185

Goldsmith Seeds, Inc. (54)
Gilroy, CA 95020

Ferry-Morse Seed Co. (55)
Box 100
Mountain View, CA 94040
Ferry-Morse varieties are available in many garden stores. They offer a 48-page booklet, Home Garden Guide. The cost is 98¢.

Petoseed Co., Inc. (56)
Box 4206
Saticoy, CA 93003

T. Sakata Seed Co. (57)
120 Montgomery St.
San Francisco, CA 94101

'Flora America' flourishes in wooden containers.

Index

Page numbers in italics indicate illustrations.